国际中文教育武术技术推广系列教材
Wushu Techniques Textbook Series for International Chinese Education

国际武术联合会
International Wushu Federation
中国武术协会
Chinese Wushu Association
北京体育大学汉语国际推广武术师资培训基地
Wushu Teacher Training Base for Chinese International Promotion of Beijing Sport University

长 拳
Chang Quan

李英奎　主编
王卓君　　译

北京体育大学出版社

策划编辑：佟　晖
责任编辑：潘海英
责任校对：赵红霞
版式设计：李　鹤

图书在版编目（CIP）数据

长拳 : 汉英对照 / 李英奎主编 ; 王卓君译. -- 北
京 : 北京体育大学出版社, 2022.6
　　ISBN 978-7-5644-3657-5

　　Ⅰ. ①长… Ⅱ. ①李… ②王… Ⅲ. ①长拳－基本知
识－汉、英 Ⅳ. ①G852.12

　　中国版本图书馆CIP数据核字(2022)第094281号

长拳
CHANGQUAN

李英奎　主编
王卓君　　译

出版发行：北京体育大学出版社
地　　址：北京市海淀区农大南路1号院2号楼2层办公B-212
邮　　编：100084
网　　址：http: //cbs.bsu.edu.cn
发行部：010-62989320
邮购部：北京体育大学出版社读者服务部 010-62989432
印　　刷：唐山玺诚印务有限公司
开　　本：710 mm × 1000 mm　　1/16
成品尺寸：170 mm × 240 mm
印　　张：15.75
字　　数：278千字
版　　次：2022年6月第1版
印　　次：2022年6月第1次印刷
定　　价：100.00元

国际中文教育武术技术推广系列教材

组织机构

教育部中外语言交流合作中心

北京体育大学

国际武术联合会

中国武术协会

审定委员会

吴　彬　门惠丰　金肖冰

编写委员会

总　主　编：李士英

副总主编：高楚兰　佟　晖

分册主编：王二平　李士英　李英奎

　　　　　林小美　高楚兰

国际中文教育武术技术推广系列教材
《长拳》编委会

主　编：李英奎

副主编：王晓娜

编　委：王世龙　刘晓玲　虞泽民

示　范：王芊千

译　者：王卓君

目录 Contents

武礼篇

Wushu Etiquette

中华武术历史悠久，源远流长，内容丰富多彩、博大精深。源于中国，属于世界的武术运动，深受世界各国人民喜爱，已成为全人类共有的精神、文化财富。

Chinese Wushu (martial arts) goes back to time immemorial, and is well-established, long-standing, and profound. Originating from China, Wushu also belongs to the world, and is greatly admired by people all over the world; it has become a spiritual and cultural asset shared by all.

一、武 礼　　Wushu Etiquette

"未曾习武先习礼"，武礼是中国传统的礼法之一。武礼现已成为在国际上一致采用的、具有代表性的、规范统一的武术标准礼法。

武礼的行礼方式包括徒手礼（抱拳礼、注目礼）、持械礼、递械礼和接械礼等。

"Before practicing Wushu, acquire relevant etiquette first." Wushu etiquette is part of China's traditional cultural rule of etiquette, and has become a common practice in the international Wushu community.

Wushu etiquette is represented by barehanded salutes (palm-fist salute; eye salute), weapon-holding salute, weapon-delivering salute, and weapon-receiving salute.

1. 抱拳礼　　　　　　　　　　　　　　　　　　　　Palm-fist Salute

　　抱拳礼的行礼方式是：并步站立，左手四指并拢伸直成掌，拇指屈拢，右手成拳，左掌心掩贴右拳面，左指根线与右拳棱相齐；左掌、右拳胸前相抱，高度与胸平齐，肘尖略下垂，拳、掌与胸间距为20~30厘米；头正，身直，目视受礼者。（图1-1）

　　抱拳礼的含义是：左掌为文，象征和平，代表武德，寓意孝敬父母、尊敬师长、爱国敬业、诚信友善、仁爱感恩、谦卑简朴；拇指弯曲表示谦虚，寓意武术源于中国，属于世界，应虚心好学、永不自大。右拳为武，象征力量，代表武技，寓意尚武崇德、追求卓越、为国争光、为民服务。左掌盖在右拳上表示爱心、礼让、止戈为武。两手相合，表示习武者要文武兼备、内外兼修，五湖四海天下武林是一家，以武会友、友好团结，弘扬武学文化，造福人类。抱拳礼的寓意为和平、团结和友谊。

The palm-fist salute is as follows: stand with your feet together; the four fingers of your left hand stay straight together as an open palm, with the thumb bent and close to the index finger; the right hand forms a fist, with knuckles pressed against the center of the left palm, and the left palm's finger base line aligned with the right fist's metacarpophalangeal joint line. The fist and palm stay together 20-30 cm away from in front of your chest, with the tips of both elbows slightly drooping. Keep your head and body upright, and gaze at the one receiving the salute. (Fig. 1-1)

The palm-fist salute means: the left palm stands for erudition, symbolizing peace and martial ethics, and implying filial piety to parents, respect for teachers, patriotism, dedication, honesty and friendliness, benevolence and gratitude, humility, and frugality; the bent thumb means modesty, implying that Wushu originates from China and belongs to the world, and that those practicing Wushu should be humble and studious, but never arrogant. The right fist stands for martial arts, symbolizing strength and skills, implying the pursuit of virtue and excellence, glory for the country, and service to the people. The left palm is covered on the right fist to express love, comity, and truce.

The fist meets the palm to indicate that those practicing Wushu must be a master of both the pen and sword, in other words, to be well versed in both polite letters and martial arts. The world's Wushu community is a big family; Wushu is practiced to meet with friends, maintain friendship and unity, and to promote Wushu culture to benefit humanity. In short, the palm-fist salute symbolizes peace, unity, and friendship.

图 1-1　抱拳礼
Fig. 1-1 Palm-fist Salute

2. 注目礼　　　　　　　　　　　　　　　　　　　　　　Eye Salute

注目礼的行礼方法是：并步站立，目视受礼者或向前平视，身体正直，以示对受礼者的恭敬、尊重。若表示答诺或聆听指教受益时，可微点头示意。

The eye salute is as follows: stand with your feet together; gaze at the recipient or look straight ahead; keep your body upright to show respect for the recipient. To respond to an eye salute, you can nod your head slightly.

3. 持械礼   Salute with a Weapon

持械礼是习练武术器械时行的礼节，礼仪内涵同"抱拳礼"。

① 持剑礼的行礼方法是：并步站立，左手持剑，屈臂，使剑身贴前臂外侧，斜横于胸前；右手拇指屈拢，成斜侧立掌（或剑指），以掌外沿附于左手食指根节，高度与胸平齐，肘微下垂，目视受礼者。（图1-2）

Saluting with a weapon is an etiquette to follow when practicing a weapon, and means the same as the palm-fist salute.

① Salute with a sword: stand with your feet together, hold the sword in your left hand, bend your arms, and the blade is attached to the outer edge of the left forearm and diagonally across the chest. Your right palm (or sword finger) stays oblique with the thumb bent, and the palm's outer edge is attached to the joint of the left hand's index finger. This position is at the height where the chest is, with the elbows slightly drooping and eyes on the recipient. (Fig. 1-2)

图 1-2　持剑礼
Fig. 1-2 Sword-holding Salute

② 抱刀礼的行礼方法是：并步站立，左手抱刀，屈臂，使刀横于胸前，刀身斜向下，刀背贴附于前臂之上，刀刃向上；右手拇指屈拢成斜侧立掌，以掌心附在左手拇指第一指节上，高度与胸平齐，肘微下垂，目视受礼者。（图1-3）

② Salute with a broadsword: stand with your feet together, hold the broadsword with your left hand, and bend your arms so that the broadsword is horizontal to the chest; the blade is slanted downward, with its spine attached to your forearm, and its belly facing upward. Your right palm stays oblique with the thumb bent, and the palm is attached to the first knuckle of the left thumb. This position is at the height where the chest is, with the elbows slightly drooping and eyes on the recipient. (Fig. 1-3)

图 1-3 抱刀礼
Fig. 1-3 Broadsword-holding Salute

③ 持枪礼的行礼方法是：并步站立，右手握枪端，屈臂于胸前，枪身直立，枪尖向上；左手拇指屈拢成侧立掌，掌心与右手指根节指面相贴，高度与胸平齐，肘略下垂，目视受礼者。

③ Salute with a spear: stand with your feet together, hold the spear in your right hand, with the arms bent in front of the chest; keep the spear upright, with its tip facing upward; keep your left palm in an oblique position with the thumb bent; the palm is in contact with the right hand's finger joints. This position is at the height where the chest is, with the elbows slightly drooping and eyes on the recipient.

④ 持棍礼的行礼方法是：并步站立，右手握棍把段（靠棍把1/3处），屈臂于胸前，棍身直立，棍梢向上；左手拇指屈拢成侧立掌，掌心与右手指根节指面相贴，高度与胸平齐，肘略下垂，目视受礼者。（图1-4）

④ Salute with a stick: stand with your feet together, hold the handle of the stick with your right hand (1/3 of the handle), with your arms bent in front of the chest; keep the stick upright, with its tip facing upward; keep your left palm in an oblique position with the thumb bent; the palm is in contact with the right hand's finger joints. This position is at the height where the chest is, with the elbows slightly drooping and eyes on the recipient. (Fig. 1-4)

图 1-4　持棍礼
Fig. 1-4 Stick-holding Salute

4. 递械礼   Weapon-delivering Salute

递械礼包括递剑礼、递刀礼、递枪礼和递棍礼等。

① 递剑礼的行礼方法是：并步站立，左手托护手盘，右手托剑前身，使剑平横于胸前，剑尖向右，目视接剑者。

② 递刀礼的行礼方法是：并步站立，左手托护手盘，右手托刀前身，使刀平横于胸前，刀刃向里，目视接刀者。

③ 递枪礼的行礼方法是：并步站立，双手靠近握枪于把段处，左手在上，两臂屈圆，使枪垂直于体前，枪尖向上，目视接枪者。

④ 递棍礼的行礼方法是：并步站立，双手靠近握棍于把段（靠棍把1/3处），左手在上，两臂屈圆，使棍垂直竖于体前，棍梢向上，目视接棍者。

其他器械的递械礼参照上述规范统一。

The weapon-delivering salute includes the sword-delivering salute, broadsword-delivering salute, spear-delivering salute, and stick-delivering salute etc.

① The sword-delivering salute is as follows: stand with your feet together, hold the cross-guard in your left hand, and support the front section of the blade with your right hand, so that the sword stays horizontal across the chest, with the tip of the sword pointing to the right and eyes on the recipient.

② The broadsword-delivering salute is as follows: stand with your feet together, hold the cross-guard in your left hand, and support the front section of the broadsword with your right hand, so that the broadsword stays horizontal across the chest, with the belly of the broadsword facing inward, and eyes on the recipient.

③ The spear-delivering salute is as follows: stand with your feet together, hold the spear with both hands close to the handle, with your left hand on top and arms rounded; the spear stays vertical in front of your body, with the spear tip facing upward and your eyes on the recipient.

④ The stick-delivering salute is as follows: stand with your feet together, keep your hands close and hold the stick by the handle (1/3 of the stick), with your left hand on top and arms rounded, so that the stick stays vertical in front of your body, with the tip of the stick facing upward and your eyes on the recipient.

For the delivering of other weapons, please refer to the above-mentioned methods.

5. 接械礼   Weapon-receiving Salute

接械礼包括接剑礼、接刀礼、接枪礼和接棍礼等。

① 接剑礼的行礼方法是：开步站立，左手掌心向上，托剑于递剑者两手之间，右手手心向下接握剑柄，目视右手，接剑。

② 接刀礼的行礼方法是：开步站立，左手掌心向上，托刀于递刀者两手之间，右手手心向下接握刀柄，目视右手，接刀。

③ 接枪礼的行礼方法是：开步站立，两手虎口向上，上下靠拢，左手在上，靠近递枪者手上部接握，目视双手，接枪。

④ 接棍礼的行礼方法是：开步站立，两手虎口向上，上下靠拢，左手在上，靠近递棍者手上部接握，目视双手，接棍。

其他器械的接械礼参照上述规范统一。

The weapon-receiving salute includes the sword-receiving salute, broadsword-receiving salute, spear-receiving salute, and stick-receiving salute etc.

① The sword-receiving salute is as follows: stand with your feet apart; your left palm faces upward and supports the sword between the deliverer's hands, and your right palm faces downward and holds the hilt of the sword; eyes on the right hand when receiving the sword.

② The broadsword receiving salute is as follows: stand with your feet apart; your left palm faces upward and supports the broadsword between the deliverer's hands, and your right palm faces downward and holds the hilt of the broadsword; eyes on the right hand when receiving the broadsword.

③ The spear-receiving salute is as follows: stand with your feet apart; the part of the hand between the thumb and the index finger faces upward; hands stay close, with your left hand above your right hand and the deliverer's hands; eyes on both hands when receiving the spear.

④ The stick-receiving salute is as follows: stand with your feet apart; the part of the hand between the thumb and the index finger faces upward; hands stay close, with your left hand above your right hand and the deliverer's hands; eyes on both hands when receiving the stick.

For the receiving of other weapons, please refer to the above-mentioned methods.

二、武礼的应用   Applying Wushu Etiquette

1. 技术教学训练课   Technical Training Sessions

队长整队完毕，向老师报告时，师生均行"注目礼"。老师向学生说"上课！"，队长发"敬礼！"口令，学生行"抱拳礼"；老师看学生都行礼端正后，行"抱拳礼"答谢，落手立正；然后学生再落手立正。礼毕，授课开始。

授课结束，队长整队完毕，老师对本节课的整体情况进行总结发言后示意队长发"敬礼！"口令，学生行"抱拳礼"；老师看学生都行礼端正后，行"抱拳礼"答谢，落手立正；然后学生再落手立正。礼毕，老师向学生说"下课！"，老师和学生同时击掌，下课。

After the team leader lines everyone up and reports to the instructor, both the instructor and students salute with their eyes. The instructor says to the students, "Class!", then the team leader gives the "Salute" instruction, and the students perform the palm-fist salute. The instructor will make sure that all students are saluting properly and respond to them with the same position. The instructor then puts down his hands and resumes the position of attention; the students will do the same. After this, the session begins.

At the end of the session, the team leader again lines everyone up, and the instructor recaps on the session and then signals the team leader to give the "Salute" instruction. Then the students perform the palm-fist salute, and the instructor will make sure that all students are saluting properly and respond to them with the same position. The instructor then puts down his hands and resumes the position of attention; the students will do the same. After this, the instructor says, "Class dismissed", and gives students a high five before they leave the class.

2. 专业理论课　　　　　　　　　　　　　　Theoretical Sessions

老师走上讲台，向学生说"上课！"，队长发"起立！敬礼！"口令，学生行"抱拳礼"；老师看学生都行礼端正后，行"抱拳礼"答谢，落手立正；然后学生再落手立正，队长发"坐下！"口令。礼毕，学生就座，授课开始。

授课结束，老师向学生说"下课！"，队长发"起立！敬礼！"口令，学生行"抱拳礼"；老师看学生都行礼端正后，行"抱拳礼"答谢，落手立正；然后学生再落手立正，队长发"坐下！"口令。礼毕，学生就座，下课。

The instructor walks up to the podium and says to the students, "Class!", and the team leader follows by shouting out "Stand up! Salute!" The students then perform the palm-fist salute. The instructor will make sure that all students are saluting properly and respond to them with the same position. The instructor then puts down his hands and resumes the position of attention; the students will do the same. The team leader then shouts out "Sit down"! After this, the students are seated, and the session begins.

At the end of the session, the instructor says, "Class dismissed". The team leader shouts out "Stand up! Salute!", then the students perform the palm-fist salute. The instructor will make sure that all students are saluting properly and respond to them with the same position. The instructor then puts down his hands and resumes the position of attention; the students will do the same. The team leader then shouts out "Sit down"! After this, the students are seated, and the session ends.

3. 武术比赛、表演等　　　　Wushu Competition and Performance

　　在武术测试、比赛时，运动员听到点名后应立即进场，面向裁判长，行"抱拳礼"或"持械礼"，待裁判长示意后，即走向起势位置；完成套路后，须并步收势，再转向裁判长行"抱拳礼"或"持械礼"，即可退场；赛后示分时应向裁判长行"抱拳礼"或"持械礼"。

　　在武术表演时，表演开始前和结束后，表演者应向主席台上的贵宾、前辈和观众行"抱拳礼"或"持械礼"。在武术的社会活动中，表演者受到介绍时应行"抱拳礼"示礼。在交流技术、切磋技艺时，双方也应行"抱拳礼"或"持械礼"。武林同道见面问候、告别时，也应行"抱拳礼"，以体现尊师重道，礼尚往来。

During tests or competitions, athletes should enter the arena immediately upon hearing their names called out, face the referee, and perform the palm-fist salute or weapon-holding salute; after the referee gestures, athletes should go to the starting position, complete the routine, stand at the finishing position, and then turn to the referee to perform the palm-fist salute or weapon-holding salute before leaving the arena. When the scores are announced, athletes should perform the palm-fist salute or weapon-holding salute to the referee.

When performing Wushu, before and after the performance, performers should do the palm-fist salute or weapon-holding salute to the distinguished guests on the rostrum, seniors, and spectators. On social occasions of Wushu, when being introduced, performers should perform the palm-fist salute to show etiquette. When exchanging techniques and discussing skills, both sides should perform the palm-fist salute or weapon-holding salute. When Wushu colleagues greet each other or say goodbye, they should also perform the palm-fist salute to show respect for the instructor and courtesy.

长拳概述

Introduction to Chang Quan

一、认识长拳　　　　　　Understanding Chang Quan

长拳是以姿势舒展、动迅静定、劲力饱满、节奏鲜明为特点的一个武术拳种。

中华人民共和国国家体育运动委员会于1952年成立后，邀请了一批武术专家和学者，以查拳、华拳、花拳、红拳、炮拳及少林拳等拳种为基础，以四击、八法、十二型为技术和技法标准，选取姿势舒展、大开大合、翻转腾跃的动作，进行重新组合和编排，编创出了被统称为"规定长拳"的甲组长拳、乙组长拳、初级长拳等套路。20世纪50年代，国家体育运动委员会根据武术自身发展的规律及社会发展的需要，把长拳作为武术竞赛项目之一，并在青少年中推广。长拳因此得到了较为广泛的普及。随后，依照武术竞赛规则的要求，运动员可以根据自己的身体素质及运动特长，编创出有别于"规定长拳"套路的"自选长拳"套路。与此同时，以拳、掌、勾为基本手型，以弓步、马步、仆步、虚步、歇步为基本步型，以腾空飞脚、腾空摆莲、旋风脚为基本跳跃动作，以提膝平衡、侧身平衡、燕式平衡为基本平衡动作的长拳基本功逐渐成为长拳项目的训练内容，并形成了稳定的训练模式。至此，现代长拳或者说是新编长拳形成了自己的体系。在一定程度上，长拳的运动形式、动作规格等有了可比性，这为长拳纳入正式比赛奠定了基础。现代长拳的产生和完善，是现代武术人集体智慧的结晶。

随着武术事业的蓬勃发展，长拳套路在动作结构、布局安排、速度、难度、腾空跳跃等方面都有了新的突破和创新。长拳运动的训练更加强调动作规格化、注重功力和加强攻防意识，长拳技术以姿势、方法、身法、眼法、精神、劲力、呼吸、节奏为八要素，提出了"高、难、美、新"的发展方向，使长拳成为深受民众喜爱的一个拳种。目前，伴随着武术套路竞赛发展起来的长拳技术体系，已经成为国际性武术比赛的主要内容。

Chang Quan is a school of Wushu boxing characterized by expansiveness and gracefulness in posture, speed in movement, full of strength, and clear rhythm.

After the establishment of the National Sports Committee of the People's Republic of China in 1952, a group of Wushu experts and scholars were invited to recombine and arrange movements with expansive postures, vigorous body changes, and somersaults, based on Cha Quan, Hua Quan, Hwa Quan, Hong Quan, Pao Quan and Shaolin Quan, and taken four skills of attacking, eight methods and twelve postures as the technical and technique standards, creating the generally called "Compulsory Routines", including Group A Chang Quan, Group B Chang Quan, Elementary Chang Quan Routine, and other routines. In the 1950s, according to the law of Wushu's development and the needs of social development, Chang Quan was prescribed as one of the Wushu competition events and got promoted among young people, which made it widely popular. Later, in accordance with the requirements of Wushu competition rules, different from the "Compulsory Routines", athletes can compile and create "Optional Routines" based on their own physical fitness and sports specialties. At the same time, the basics of Chang Quan, which include basic hand forms: fist, palm, and hook; basic stances: bow stance, horse stance, crouching stance, empty stance, and resting stance; basic jumping exercises: flying front kick, jump and outward swing kick, and Tornado kick; and basic balance skills: knee-raised balance, sideway balance, and swallow balance, have gradually become the training content, thus forming a stable training mode. In this context, the contemporary Chang Quan or New Chang Quan has formed its own system. To some extent, the sports movements and their indicators become comparable, which lays the foundation for Chang Quan's inclusion in official competitions. The emergence and perfection of contemporary Chang Quan is the crystallization of the collective wisdom of modern Wushu practitioners.

With the vigorous development of Wushu, Chang Quan routines have made breakthroughs and innovations in movement structure, arrangement, speed, difficulty, and jumping techniques. The training of Chang Quan emphasizes more on the standardization of movements, techniques and skills, and the awareness of attack and defense. Focusing on eight elements: posture, methods, body movement, expression in the eyes, spirit, strength, breathing and tempo, Chang Quan techniques are developing in the proposed direction featuring "expertise, challenges, beauty and innovation", making itself a kind of boxing deeply loved by the people. At present, the technical system of Chang Quan developed along with Wushu taolu competitions has become the main content of international Wushu competitions.

二、长拳运动特点　　Characteristics of Chang Quan

长拳运动强调人体的内外合一，要求内部的精神、气息、劲力与表现于外的静型和动态协调一致。练习长拳要求全神贯注，将攻防意识贯注于动作，并通过眼神的配合表现出来。长拳运动要求"劲力顺达"。顺，就是要符合人体运动的规律，而且动作与意识、气息要配合一致。达，就是要让力量达到攻击的目标。为此，在劲力运用技法方面，要刚柔相兼，既不能一味地刚而形成僵劲，也不能一味地柔而失去长拳的特点。同时，要注重通过瞬间爆发的"寸劲"，表现出准确的力点，展示出"力达"的演练效果。

Chang Quan is an integral movement that emphasizes the unity of the inside and outside of the human body. It requires the harmony between the spirit, breath and strength of the inside and the static and dynamic performance of the outside. Practicing Chang Quan requires full concentration. You should focus on the attack and defense awareness in the movement, and then express it through the cooperation of your eyes. In Chang Quan exercise, the strength must be smooth. Shun (smoothness) means the mind and breath must coordinate well with each other conforming to the laws of body movement. Da (reaching) is to make the force reach the target of the attack. Therefore, for strength techniques, it is necessary to combine both rigidity and softness. It cannot be blindly rigid and become inflexible, nor blindly soft and lose the characteristics of Chang Quan. At the same time, you should pay attention to the accurate force point through the sudden burst of "appropriate strength", demonstrating that the force is reached and effective.

1. 姿势正确 Correct Postures

长拳套路是由诸多动作有机地衔接组成的。无论是动态还是静型，长拳套路对身体各部分的姿势都有一定的规格要求，要求做到"势正招圆"。

"势"通常是指各种静止姿势。基本要求是头正、颈直、沉肩、挺胸、立腰、敛臀，上肢动作要挺拔；下肢动作要稳健、匀称、轮廓清楚。

"招"主要是指由动到静的运动过程，一个完整的技术方法。它不仅要求做到有头有尾，过程清楚，而且要求身体各部位高度协调、圆满、完整，各种拳法、掌法、步法、身法的变化路线清晰、力点准确、攻防有序。

Chang Quan routines are composed of many systematically connected movements. Whether they are dynamic or static, there are certain specifications for the posture requirements of each part of the body, and it is required to achieve "Shizheng Zhaoyuan"(accurate postures and complete movements).

"Shi" usually refers to various static postures. The basic requirements are head upright, nape straight, shoulders dropped, chest out, waist straight, and hips tucked, i.e. the upper limb movements should be straight and the lower limb movements should be steady, well-balanced and clear in outline.

"Zhao" mainly refers to the movment process from dynamic to static, a complete technical method. It requires not only a clear route from the beginning to the end, but also a high degree of coordination, perfection, and integrity of all parts of the body. Changes in various boxing techniques, palm techniques, footwork, and body techniques should ensure clear routes, accurate force points, and orderly attack and defense.

2. 舒展大方　　　　　　　　　　Expansiveness and Gracefulness

长拳的姿势要求头正、颈直、沉肩、挺胸、立腰，动作舒展大方。舒展大方体现在头、臂、腰、腿各部位在完成一个动作时路线的幅度要大。在完成这些动作时，起止点、路线、力点都要清晰、准确，应充分体现出动作的攻防特点。

The posture requirements for Chang Quan include head upright, nape straight, shoulders dropped, chest high and waist straight. The movements should be expansive and graceful, which means that the head, arms, the waist and legs should have a larger range of routes when completing movements. In doing so, the starting and ending points, routes, and force points should be clear and accurate, which can fully illustrare the offensive and defensive characteristics of the movements.

3. 动作灵活　　　　　　　　　　Flexible Body Movements

长拳运动身法多样，闪、展、腾、挪、起伏、转折等动作变化在躯干的紧密、协调配合下，完整一体。动作灵活体现在头、臂、腰、腿各部位在完成一个动作时路线的幅度要大、节奏的变化要快。

In Chang Quan, there are various body movement techniques, such as Shan (dodging), Zhan (stretching), Teng (leaping), Nuo (moving), Qifu (rising and falling), Zhuanzhe (turning) etc., all of which are integrated with the close cooperation of the torso. The flexibility of the movement is reflected in the fact that the head, arms, the waist and legs should have a larger range of routes and rapid changes in rhythm when completing movements.

4. 快速有力   Quickness and Full of Power

长拳的运动特点，一般是有动有静的，既有招，又有势。"静如处女，动如脱兔"，不动则已，一动就要非常迅速有力。

The characteristics of Chang Quan are generally dynamic as well as static, containing both "Zhao" and "Shi". As the saying goes "Quiet like a virgin, moving like a rabbit". If you don't move, you can be static; once you move, you shoud move very quickly and forcefully.

5. 节奏鲜明   Clear Tempo

长拳运动因节奏鲜明而富有感染力和生气。动作、组合、段落之间所表现的韵律变化，应恰如其分。整套动作，既要在快速中进行，又要通过速度、力量的变化，有机地处理刚与柔、动与静、轻与重、疾与缓等演练技巧。

Chang Quan is full of appeal and vitality because of its clear tempo. The rhythmic changes between movements, combinations, and segments should be appropriate. The whole set of movements should not only be carried out fast, but also through the changes of speed and strength, to get the hang of the dynamics between: rigidity and softness; motion and stillness; lightness and heaviness; swiftness and slowness.

长拳基本动作

Basic Movements of Chang Quan

一、抱拳礼 Palm-fist Salute

抱拳礼的行礼方式是：并步站立，左手四指并拢伸直成掌，拇指屈拢，右手成拳，左掌心掩贴右拳面，左指根线与右拳棱相齐；左掌、右拳胸前相抱，高度与胸平齐，肘尖略下垂，拳、掌与胸间距为20～30厘米；头正，身直，目视受礼者。（图3-1）

要点：右拳眼斜对胸窝，肘尖略下垂，掌、拳与胸部的距离为20～30厘米。

The palm-fist salute is as follows: stand with your feet together; the four fingers of your left hand stay straight together as an open palm, with the thumb bent and close to the index finger; the right hand forms a fist, with knuckles pressed against the center of the left palm, and the left palm's finger base line aligned with the right fist's metacarpophalangeal joint line. The fist and palm stay together 20-30 cm away from in front of your chest, with the tips of both elbows slightly drooping. Keep your head and body upright, and gaze at the one receiving the salute. (Fig. 3-1)

Key Points: The eye of the right fist is slanted towards the chest socket, the tip of the elbow is slightly drooping, and the distance between the palm, fist and the chest is 20-30 cm.

图 3-1　抱拳礼
Fig. 3-1 Palm-fist Salute

二、柔 韧 Flexibility

1.横竖叉 Side Split and Front Split

（1）横叉

开步站立。两腿屈膝下蹲，两掌体前触地，指尖向前，五指自然分开；两腿向左、右两侧分开，蹬膝伸直，两腿内侧着地，脚尖向前。（图3-2）

要点：髋关节放松，两膝伸直，两腿贴于地面。

(1) Side Split

Stand upright with feet apart, bend your legs and squat down. Your plams touch the ground in front of you with fingertips facing forward and five fingers naturally separated. The legs are separated on both sides of the body, with the knees straightened, the inside of the legs on the ground, and the toes facing forward. (Fig. 3-2)

Key Points: Relax your hips, straighten your knees, and keep your legs on the ground.

图 3-2　横叉
Fig. 3-2 Side Split

（2）竖叉

并步站立。左脚向前上步，随即左脚尖勾起、向上；右脚向后退步，右腿内侧着地，脚尖向右；两掌分别上摆至左、右两侧，与肩同高，指尖向上；目视前方。左右腿轮换练习。（图3-3）

要点：两膝伸直，上体保持正直。

(2) Front Split

Stand upright with feet together. Step forward with the left foot, and then raise the toes of the left upward; step backward with the right foot, with the inside of the right leg on the ground and the toes facing to the right; swing the palms to the left and right side respectively, at the height of the shoulders, with the fingertips pointing upwards; look straight ahead. Practice in turns with the left and right leg. (Fig. 3-3)

Key Points: Keep your knees straight and your upper body straight.

图 3-3　竖叉
Fig. 3-3　Front Split

2. 过肩   Shoulder Pass-through Stretch with a Stick

开步站立。两手握棍于体前，虎口相对；以肩关节为轴，两肘伸直，两手握棍向前、向上经头部向后旋转至体后；目视前方。（图3-4）

要点：两肘伸直，握棍距离保持不变。

Stand upright with feet apart. Hold the stick in front of the body with both hands, the part of the hand between the thumb and the index finger facing each other; take the shoulder joint as the axis, straighten both elbows, and use both hands to hold the stick horizontally from a forward to an upward position, wielding it over your head and swiveling it backward to the back of your body; look straight ahead. (Fig. 3-4)

Key Points: Straighten your elbows and keep the distance unchanged when you hold the stick.

图 3-4　过肩
Fig. 3-4 Shoulder Pass-through Stretch with a Stick

3. 下腰   Backbend

开步站立。两臂伸直上举，掌心向前，指尖向上；目视前方。上体后仰，两掌撑地，上肢与下肢呈拱桥形。（图3-5）

要点：挺胸、挺髋、展腹、抬头，手触地时腰向上顶，两脚跟不得离地。

Stand upright with feet apart. Extend your arms straight upward, palms forward, fingertips up; look straight ahead. Lean the upper body backward until two palms are on the ground, making the upper and lower limbs in the shape of an arch bridge. (Fig. 3-5)

Key Points: Keep your chest out, hips out, belly out, and head up. When your hands touch the ground, your waist should go up, and your heels should not be off the ground.

图 3-5　下腰
Fig. 3-5 Backbend

三、手 型 Hand Forms

1.拳 Fist

四指（食指、中指、无名指、小指）并拢卷握，拇指紧扣食指和中指的第二指节（图3-6）。拳心向下为平拳，拳眼向上为立拳。

要点：拳要握紧，拳面要平，腕部伸直。

Four fingers (index finger, middle finger, ring finger, little finger) are closed into a fist with the thumb over the second knuckle of the index finger and the middle finger (Fig. 3-6). When the center of fist faces downward, it is called Ping Quan (even fist); when the eye of fist faces upward, it is called Li Quan (upward fist).

Key Points: Hold the fist tightly, with the face of fist even and the wrist unbent.

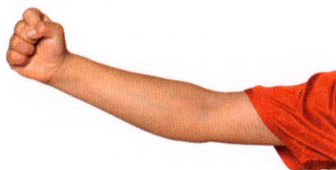

图3-6 拳
Fig. 3-6 Fist

2.掌   Palm

四指（食指、中指、无名指、小指）伸直并拢，拇指弯曲紧扣于虎口处。（图3-7）

要点：四指伸直并拢，拇指紧扣一侧。

Four fingers (index finger, middle finger, ring finger, little finger) stay straight together, and the thumb is bent and pressed onto the part between the thumb and the index finger. (Fig. 3-7)

Key Points: Put four fingers straight together, and cling the thumb onto one side of the palm.

图 3-7 掌
Fig. 3-7 Palm

3.勾   Hook

五指指尖捏紧并拢，屈腕。（图3-8）

要点：屈腕用力。

Pinch the tips of five fingers together, with the wrist bent. (Fig. 3-8)

Key Points: Bend your wrist with foce.

图 3-8 勾
Fig. 3-8 Hook

四、步 型 — Stances

1. 弓步 — Bow Stance

并步站立。左脚向前上步，屈膝半蹲，大腿呈水平位，脚尖微内扣，膝垂直于脚面；右腿挺膝伸直，脚尖内扣斜向前方；两脚全脚掌着地，此为左弓步（图3-9）。右脚在前为右弓步。

要点：左腿大腿呈水平位，膝垂直于脚面，全脚掌着地；右脚脚尖内扣。

Stand upright with feet together. Step forward with the left foot, and bend the knee to form a half squat, with the thigh at horizontal level, the toes slightly buckled in, and the knee perpendicular to the foot; straighten the right leg with the toes pointing inward and the foot turning obliquely forwards; the soles of both feet are on the ground. This is the left bow stance, and the right foot in the front forms the right bow stance. (Fig. 3-9)

Key Points: The left thigh is at horizontal level, the knee is perpendicular to the instep, and the sole of the foot is on the ground. The toes of the right foot point inward.

图 3-9　弓步
Fig. 3-9 Bow Stance

2. 马步   Horse Stance

　　并步站立。左脚向左开步（两脚间距约为脚长的3倍），两腿屈膝半蹲，大腿呈水平位，两膝外撑，脚尖向前，两脚全脚掌着地。（图3-10）

　　要点：屈膝坐髋，大腿呈水平位，躯干微前倾，两脚间距不宜过小，全脚掌着地，脚尖向前。

Stand upright with feet together. Step to the left with the left foot (the distance between the feet is about three times the length of the foot). Bend the knees to form a half squat with both legs, the thighs at horizontal level, the knees outwardly supported, and the toes facing forward. The soles of both feet are on the ground. (Fig. 3-10)

Key Points: Bend the knees and drop the hips with the thighs at horizontal level and the torso leaning forward slightly; the distance between your feet should not be too narrow, and the soles of your feet should be on the ground with toes pointing forward.

图 3-10　马步
Fig. 3-10 Horse Stance

3. 仆步 Crouching Stance

并步站立。左脚向左横开步，左腿平铺伸直，脚尖内扣；右腿屈膝全蹲，臀部紧贴小腿，膝与脚尖外展，两脚全脚掌着地，此为左仆步（图3-11）。左腿屈膝，右腿平铺为右仆步。

要点：屈蹲腿全蹲，平铺腿伸直，平铺腿全脚掌内扣着地。

Stand upright with feet together. Step to the left with the left foot, and straighten the left leg to approach the ground with toes pointing inward; bend the right knee to make a full squat with buttocks close to the calf, the knees and toes outstretched, and the soles of both feet on the ground; this is the left crouching stance. If you bend the left leg and straighten the right leg to approach the ground, that is the right crouching stance. (Fig. 3-11)

Key Points: Keep a full squat with the squatting leg. Straighten the stretching leg to approach the ground. The sole of the stretching leg buckles inward on the ground.

图 3-11 仆步
Fig. 3-11 Crouching Stance

4. 虚步   Empty Stance

并步站立。右脚尖外展约45°，右腿屈膝半蹲，左腿微屈膝前伸，左脚尖内侧向前虚点地面；身体重心落于右腿，此为左虚步（图3-12）。右脚尖向前虚点地面为右虚步。

要点：屈蹲腿大腿呈水平位，全脚掌着地；身体重心落于右腿。

Stand upright with feet together. When the right toes stretch outward about 45°, bend the right leg to form a half squat. Slightly bend the left leg forward, and the inner side of the left toes slightly touch the ground with the center of gravity falling on the right leg. This is the left empty stance (Fig. 3-12). If the right toes slightly touch the ground, that is the right empty stance.

Key Points: The thigh of the squatting leg is at horizontal level with the sole of the foot on the ground. The center of gravity falls on the right leg.

图 3-12 虚步
Fig. 3-12 Empty Stance

5. 歇步   Resting Stance

　　并步站立。左腿支撑，右腿经左腿后部向左后方插步，前脚掌着地，两腿交叉屈膝全蹲，左脚全脚掌着地；右脚跟离地，臀部坐于右小腿接近脚跟处，此为左歇步（图3-13）。右腿在前为右歇步。

　　要点：两腿交叉靠拢，臀部贴坐小腿。

Stand upright with feet together. Supported by the left leg, step backward to the left rear with the right leg through the back of the left leg, with the sole of the front foot touching the ground, and squat with the knees crossed and the sole of the left foot on the ground; lift the heel of the right foot off the ground, and sit with the buttocks on the right calf close to the heel; this is the left resting stance (Fig. 3-13). If the right leg is in the front, that is the right resting stance.

Key Points: Cross your legs together, and sit with your buttocks against your calves.

图 3-13　歇步
Fig. 3-13 Resting Stance

6. 坐盘 Cross-legged Sitting

　　并步站立。左腿支撑，右腿稍抬起经左小腿后向左后方插步，随即两腿交叉屈膝贴坐地面，臀部、右腿外侧及右脚背贴于地面，左小腿外侧贴近右腿外侧，此为左坐盘（图3-14）。右腿在前为右坐盘。

　　要点：两腿交叉紧贴，贴坐地面。

Stand upright with feet together. To do a left cross-legged sitting, supported by the left leg, the right leg is slightly lifted to cross through the back of the left leg to the left rear, then both legs are crossed and knees are bent to sit on the ground, with buttocks, the outside of the right leg, and the back of the right foot on the ground, the outside of the left calf close to the outside of the right leg (Fig. 3-14). If the right leg is in the front, that is the right cross-legged sitting.

Key Points: Cross your legs tightly and sit on the ground.

图 3-14　坐盘
Fig. 3-14 Cross-legged Sitting

7. 叉步   Y-shaped Stance

并步站立。左腿支撑，大腿呈水平位；右腿经左腿后部向左后方插出，前脚掌着地，右膝伸直，此为左叉步（图3-15）。右腿在前为右叉步。

要点：左腿大腿呈水平位，膝垂直于脚面，全脚掌着地；右脚前脚掌着地。

Stand upright with feet together. To do a left Y-shaped stance, supported by the left leg with the thigh in a horizontal position, step backward to the left rear with the right leg through the back of the left leg, with the forefoot on the ground and the right knee straight (Fig. 3-15). If the right leg is in the front, it is the right Y-shaped stance.

Key Points: Keep the left thigh at horizontal level, the knee perpendicular to the instep, and the sole of the foot on the ground; keep the forefoot of the right foot on the ground.

图 3-15 叉步
Fig. 3-15 Y-shaped Stance

8. 丁步 T-stance

并步站立。两腿屈膝半蹲，右脚全脚掌着地；左脚脚跟提起，脚尖点地，此为左丁步（图3-16）。右脚尖点地为右丁步。

要点：重心偏于支撑腿，一脚脚尖在另一脚内侧点地。

Stand upright with feet together. To form a left T-stance, bend both knees to form a half squat with the sole of the right foot on the ground, the left heel raised and the toes on the ground (Fig. 3-16). If the right toes touch the ground, it is the right T-stance.

Key Points: The center of gravity is on the supporting leg, and the toes of one foot touch the ground on the inside of the other foot.

图 3-16　丁步
Fig. 3-16 T-stance

长拳动作技法

Techniques of Chang Quan

一、拳 法   Fist Techniques

1.冲拳   Punching Fist

开步站立。两拳收抱于腰间，拳心向上；目视前方。右臂内旋随即右拳向前直臂冲出，拳心向下，与肩同高；目视前方。（图4-1）

要点：手臂贴肋向前，力达拳面。

Stand upright with feet apart. Hold two fists to the waist with the fist heart facing upward and eyes looking straight ahead. Turn the right arm inward, and then thrust the right fist forward forcibly with the fist heart facing downwards at the height of the shoulder, eyes looking straight ahead. (Fig. 4-1)

Key Points: Thrust the arm forward along the ribs, with the force reaching the foremost part of the fist.

图 4-1 冲拳
Fig. 4-1 Punching Fist

2. 劈拳   Chopping Fist

开步站立。两拳收抱于腰间，拳心向上；目视前方。右拳体前由下向左、向上抡臂至头上方，随即向右劈出，拳心向前，与肩同高；目视右方。（图4-2）

要点：拳自上向下劈落，直臂，力达拳轮。

Stand upright with feet apart. Hold two fists to the waist with the fist heart facing upward and eyes looking straight ahead. Move the right fist from a downward position to the left side in front of the body, swing the arm over the head, and then strike it down to the right, with the fist heart facing forward at the height of the shoulder and eyes looking to the right. (Fig. 4-2)

Key Points: Chop the fist down from top to bottom with the straight arm, and the force reaches the curve of fist.

图 4-2　劈拳
Fig. 4-2　Chopping Fist

3. 砸拳   Hammer Striking Fist

并步站立。左腿支撑，右腿屈膝上抬，右掌变拳向上冲出，拳面向上，拳心向左，左掌摆身至体左侧，掌心向左，指尖向上，与肩同高；目视前方。随即右脚下落，两腿同时屈膝，并步震脚，右拳随屈臂向下砸至腹前，左掌摆至腹前托住右拳背；目视右拳。（图4-3）

要点：拳由上向下随屈臂下砸，拳心向上，力达拳背。

Stand upright with feet together. Supported by the left leg, bend the knee and lift the right leg up. Turn the right palm into a fist and thrush it upwards with the face of fist up and the fist heart to the left. Swing the left palm to the left side of the body at the height of the shoulder, with the palm to the left, fingertips up, and eyes looking ahead. Then drop the right foot, bend the knees with both feet together and shake the feet at the same time. Bend the right arm with the fist striking down to the front of the abdomen, and swing the left palm to the front of the abdomen, holding the back of the right fist and eyes looking at the right fist. (Fig. 4-3)

Key Points: Smash the fist down from the top with the arm bent, fist heart upward, and the force reaching the back of fist.

图 4-3 砸拳
Fig. 4-3 Hammer Striking Fist

4. 栽拳   Plunging Fist

开步站立。两拳收抱于腰间，拳心向上；目视前方。左拳向前弧形上摆，拳心向上，随即内旋向左斜下方下落，拳面向下，肘微屈；目视左拳。（图4-4）

要点：臂由弯曲至伸直，拳面向下，力达拳面。

Stand upright with feet apart. Hold two fists to the waist with the fist heart facing upward and eyes looking straight ahead. The left fist swings forward in an arc, with the heart of fist facing upward, then inwardly rotates and falls diagonally downward to the left, with the fist facing down, the elbow slightly bent and eyes looking at the left fist. (Fig. 4-4)

Key Points: The fist turns from bent to straight with the face of fist down, and the force reaches the face of fist.

图 4-4　栽拳
Fig. 4-4 Plunging Fist

5. 贯拳   Sweeping Side Punch

开步站立。两拳收抱于腰间，拳心向上；目视前方。右臂内旋由右下方向前上方弧形横打，臂微屈，拳眼斜向下；目视右拳。（图4-5）

要点：转腰顺肩，力达拳面。

Stand upright with feet apart. Hold two fists to the waist with the fist heart facing upward and eyes looking straight ahead. Turn the right arm inward and hit from the lower right to the upper front in a lateral arc with the arm slightly bent, the eye of fist slanted downward, and eyes looking at the right fist. (Fig. 4-5)

Key Points: You need to turn your waist, deliver your shoulder and make the force reach the face of fist.

图 4-5　贯拳
Fig. 4-5 Sweeping Side Punch

6.撩拳   Upper-cutting Fist

开步站立。两拳收抱于腰间，拳心向上；目视前方。右拳向前上方弧形直臂撩击，拳心向左；目视前方。（图4-6）

要点：臂自下向前上方弧形直臂撩击，力达拳眼。

Stand upright with feet apart. Hold two fists to the waist with the fist heart facing upward and eyes looking straight ahead. Strike the right fist in an arc to the upper front position with a straight arm, with the heart of fist to the left and eyes looking straight ahead. (Fig. 4-6)

Key Points: Strike the straight arm in an arc from a lower position to the upper front position with the force reaching the eye of fist.

图 4-6　撩拳
Fig. 4-6 Upper-cutting Fist

7. 抄拳   Upward Fist

开步站立。两拳收抱于腰间，拳心向上；目视前方。右拳向前、向上抄起击打，拳面向前上方，与鼻同高；目视右拳。（图4-7）

要点：抄拳迅速，力达拳面。

Stand upright with feet apart. Hold two fists to the waist with the fist heart facing upward and eyes looking straight ahead. Strike the right fist forward and upward, with the fist facing upper front at the same height of the nose, and eyes looking at the right fist. (Fig. 4-7)

Key Points: Make the upward fist fast, and let the force reach the face of fist.

图 4-7　抄拳
Fig. 4-7 Upward Fist

二、掌 法 {#palm} Palm Techniques

1. 推掌 Pushing Palm

开步站立。两掌上提至两腰间，掌心向上；目视前方。右臂向前，随即内旋后右掌向前直臂推出，掌心向左斜前方，指尖向上，与肩同高；目视右掌。（图4-8）

要点：立掌向前推击，力达掌外沿。

Stand upright with feet apart. Raise two palms to the waist, palms up and eyes looking straight ahead. Throw the right arm forward. After you turn it inward, push the right palm forward with the straight arm. The palm is inclined forward to the left, the fingertips are upward at the height of the shoulder, and eyes look at the right palm. (Fig. 4-8)

Key Points: Push the arm forward with the standing palm, making the force reach the outer edge of the palm.

图 4-8 推掌
Fig. 4-8 Pushing Palm

2.挑掌   Uplifting Palm

开步站立。两掌上提至两腰间，掌心向上；目视前方。右掌由下向前抖腕挑起，与肩同高，掌心向左斜前方，指尖向上；目视右掌。（图4-9）

要点：臂由下向上塌腕上挑，力达四指。

Stand upright with feet apart. Raise two palms to the waist, palms up and eyes looking straight ahead. Uplift the right palm from a lower position to the front, shake the wrist, and show the palm at the shoulder level. The palm is inclined forward to the left with fingertips upward and eyes looking at the right palm. (Fig. 4-9)

Key Points: Raise the arm from downward to upward and press the wrist downward with the force up to four fingers.

图 4-9 挑掌
Fig. 4-9 Uplifting Palm

3. 穿掌   Thrusting Palm

左脚向左开步，前脚掌着地，上体右转；同时，右掌上提至右腰间，掌心向上，左掌摆至体前，掌心向下，肘微屈；随即右掌经左掌背向右上方穿出，掌心向上，左掌回收至右腋下；目视右掌。（图4-10）

要点： 动作连贯，力达指尖。

Step to the left with the left foot, the forefoot touches the ground, and the upper body turns to the right; at the same time, the right palm is raised to the waist on the right side, with the center of palm facing upward; the left palm is swung to the front of the body, with the center of palm facing downward and the elbow slightly bent; then the right palm is thrusted forward over the back of left palm to the upper right, with the center of palm facing upward, and the left palm is retracted to the right armpit, with eyes looking at the right palm. (Fig. 4-10)

Key Points: Movements should be smoothly connected with the force up to fingertips.

图 4-10 穿掌
Fig. 4-10 Thrusting Palm

4. 劈掌   Hacking Palm

开步站立。两拳收抱于腰间，拳心向上；目视前方。右拳变掌由右向上划弧至头上方，掌心向左，随即向前劈落，指尖向前，与肩同高；目视右掌。（图4-11）

要点：掌由上向下侧掌劈落，直臂，力达掌外沿。

Stand upright with feet apart. Hold two fists to the waist with the fist heart facing upward and eyes looking straight ahead. Turn the right fist into the palm and swing the arm in an arc from the right upward to the top of the head, with the center of palm facing to the left, and then hack the palm forward at the shoulder level, with the fingertips facing forward and eyes looking at the right palm. (Fig. 4-11)

Key Points: Hack the side palm down from the top, with a straight arm and the force reaching the outer edge of the palm.

图 4-11 劈掌
Fig. 4-11 Hacking Palm

5. 撩掌　　　　　　　　　　　　　　　　　　　　Scooping Palm

开步站立。两拳收抱于腰间，拳心向上；目视前方。右拳变掌向下、向前直臂撩出；目视右掌。（图4-12）

要点：直臂前撩，力达掌心。

Stand upright with feet apart. Hold two fists to the waist with the fist heart facing upward and eyes looking straight ahead. Turn the right fist into the palm then swiftly strike it out with the straight arm from downward to forward, eyes looking at the right palm. (Fig. 4-12)

Key Points: Strike the straight arm forward with the force reaching the center of palm.

图 4-12　撩掌
Fig. 4-12 Scooping Palm

6. 砍掌　　　　　　　　　　　　　　　　　　　　　Chopping Palm

开步站立。两拳收抱于腰间，拳心向上；目视前方。右拳变掌由右向前下方斜向发力；目视右掌。（图4-13）

要点：发力短促，力达掌外沿。

Stand upright with feet apart. Hold two fists to the waist with the fist heart facing upward and eyes looking straight ahead. Turn the right fist into the palm, and thrust it forcibly from the right to the downward front with eyes looking at the right palm. (Fig. 4-13)

Key Points: The force should be short and powerful, reaching the outer edge of the palm.

图 4-13　砍掌
Fig. 4-13 Chopping Palm

7. 亮掌   Showing Palm

开步站立。两拳收抱于腰间，拳心向上；目视前方。右拳变掌沿身体右侧向上划弧至头上方，屈肘抖腕、亮掌，掌心向上，指尖向左；目视左侧。（图4-14）

要点：抖腕亮掌，亮掌与摆头动作协调一致。

Stand upright with feet apart. Hold two fists to the waist with the fist heart facing upward and eyes looking straight ahead. Turn the right fist into the palm and draw an arc with the arm, moving it upward along the right side of the body to the top of the head, bend the elbow, shake the wrist, and show the palm up, with fingertips to the left, and eyes looking to the left. (Fig. 4-14)

Key Points: When shaking the wrist and showing the palm, palm showing should coordinate with head turning.

图 4-14　亮掌
Fig. 4-14 Showing Palm

8. 按掌 Pressing Palm

开步站立。两拳收抱于腰间，拳心向上；目视前方。右拳变掌由右向上经体前划弧下按至腹前，掌心向下，指尖向左；目视右掌。（图4-15）

要点：由上向下按压，掌心向下，力达掌心。

Stand upright with feet apart. Hold two fists to the waist with the fist heart facing upward and eyes looking straight ahead. Turn the right fist into the palm, swing it in an arc from the right to the top in front of the body and press it down to the front of the abdomen, with the center of palm facing downward, the fingertips to the left and eyes looking at the right palm. (Fig. 4-15)

Key Points: Press the palm down from the top, with the center of palm facing downward and the force reaching the palm.

图 4-15 按掌
Fig. 4-15 Pressing Palm

9. 插掌   Downward Thrusting Palm

开步站立。两拳收抱于腰间，拳心向上；目视前方。右拳变掌向前下方插出，掌心向左；目视右掌。（图4-16）

要点：臂由屈至伸，掌向下或斜下插出，直腕，力达指尖。

Stand upright with feet apart. Hold two fists to the waist with the fist heart facing upward and eyes looking straight ahead. Turn the right fist into the palm and thrust it to the lower front, with the palm to the left and eyes looking at the right palm. (Fig. 4-16)

Key Points: Turn the arm from bent to full extension. Thrust the palm downward or obliquely downward, with the wrist straight and the force reaching the fingertips.

图 4-16 插掌
Fig. 4-16 Downward Thrusting Palm

三、肘 法 Elbow Techniques

1.顶肘 Pushing Elbow

并步站立。右脚向右开步，同时，左掌向上摆至身体左侧，与肩同高，掌心向上，指尖向左，右臂屈肘，右掌摆至左胸前，掌心向上，指尖向左；目视左掌。随即右肘向右顶出，同时右臂内旋，右掌变拳，与肩同高，左臂屈肘，左掌回收至右拳面，掌心向右，指尖向上；目视右侧。（图4-17）

要点：顶肘力达肘尖，顶肘、摆头动作协调一致。

Stand upright with feet together. Step to the right with the right foot. At the same time, swing the left palm up to the left side of the body at the height of the shoulder, with the palm up and fingertips to the left. Bend the right elbow and swing the right palm to the chest, with the palm up and fingertips to the left. Your eyes look at the left palm. Then, the right elbow is pushed out to the right; at the same time, the right palm is rotated inward and turned into a fist at the height of the shoulder. Bend the left elbow and withdraw the left palm to the right fist, with the center of palm to the right, fingertips up, and eyes looking to the right. (Fig. 4-17)

Key Points: When pushing the elbow, the force reaches the end of elbow, and elbow pushing should cooperate well with head turning.

图 4-17　顶肘
Fig. 4-17 Pushing Elbow

2. 盘肘   Hook Elbow

开步站立。两拳收抱于腰间，拳心向上；目视前方。右臂由右向体前内旋后屈肘回收于胸前，拳心向下；目视前方。（图4-18）

要点：前臂由外向内盘肘，力达前臂，上臂与前臂挟紧。

Stand upright with feet apart. Hold two fists to the waist with the fist heart facing upward and eyes looking straight ahead. Revolve the right arm inward from the right to the front of the body, and then bend the elbow and retract it in front of the chest, with the center of fist downward and eyes looking straight ahead. (Fig. 4-18)

Key Points: When moving the forearm from an outward to an inward position to form a hook elbow, the force reaches the forearm, and the upper arm and the forearm are held tightly together.

图 4-18 盘肘
Fig. 4-18 Hook Elbow

3. 挎肘　　　　　　　　　　　　　　　　　　　Bending Elbow

开步站立。两拳收抱于腰间，拳心向上；目视前方。右拳由下向前、向上屈肘划弧，肘尖向下，拳心向左；目视前方。（图4-19）

要点：屈肘，拳由下向上划弧，动作迅速有力。

Stand upright with feet apart. Hold two fists to the waist with the fist heart facing upward and eyes looking straight ahead. Bend the right elbow and draw an arc with the right fist, moving it from a lower position to the upper front, with the tip of elbow downward, the heart of fist to the left and eyes looking straight ahead. (Fig. 4-19)

Key Points: Bend the elbow and swing the fist in an arc from downward to upward quickly and powerfully.

图 4-19　挎肘
Fig. 4-19 Bending Elbow

4. 格肘　　　　　　　　　　　　　　　　　　　Blocking Elbow

开步站立。两拳收抱于腰间，拳心向上；目视前方。右前臂上屈至体前向右格打；目视右拳。（图4-20）

要点：力在前臂，向内横拨为里格，向外横拨为外格。

Stand upright with feet apart. Hold two fists to the waist with the fist heart facing upward and eyes looking straight ahead. Bend the right forearm up to the front of the body and strike it to the right, with eyes looking to the right. (Fig. 4-20)

Key Points: Keep the force on the forearm. Spinning horizontally inward is called shove aside inward, and spinning horizontally outward is called shove aside outward.

图 4-20　格肘
Fig. 4-20 Blocking Elbow

5. 架肘   Parry with Elbow

开步站立。两拳收抱于腰间，拳心向上；目视前方。右臂屈臂上举，前臂横架至头前上方，拳心向前；目视前方。（图4-21）

要点：上架迅速。

Stand upright with feet apart. Hold two fists to the waist with the fist heart facing upward and eyes looking straight ahead. Lift the right arm with the elbow bent and the forearm is crossly parried to the upper front of the head, with the fist forward and eyes looking straight ahead. (Fig. 4-21)

Key Points: Parry with elbow quickly.

图 4-21　架肘
Fig. 4-21 Parry with Elbow

四、腿 法 Leg Techniques

1. 正踢腿 Front Kick

并步站立。两掌向身体两侧推出，指尖向上；目视前方。左脚向前上步，重心前移，右脚勾起向前、向上踢至前额，随即右脚向下落至左脚内侧；目视前方。（图4-22）

要点：左腿伸直，全脚掌着地；右腿伸直，脚尖勾起前踢，接近前额；上体保持正直。

Stand upright with feet together. Push the palms out to both sides of the body with the fingertips upward and eyes looking straight ahead. Step forward with the left foot, and shift the center of gravity forward. Lift the right foot forward, kick it up to the forehead with the toes hooked, then drop the right foot down to the inside of the left foot with eyes looking straight ahead. (Fig. 4-22)

Key Points: Straighten the left leg with the sole of the foot on the ground; straighten the right leg, kick the toes up close to the forehead, and keep the upper body straight.

图 4-22 正踢腿
Fig. 4-22 Front Kick

2. 斜踢腿 Oblique Kick

并步站立。两掌向身体两侧推出，指尖向上；目视前方。左脚向前上步，重心前移，右脚勾起向前、向上踢至头的左侧，随即右脚向下落至左脚内侧；目视前方。（图4-23）

要点：支撑腿伸直，全脚掌着地；斜踢腿伸直，勾脚踢向异侧耳边；上体保持正直。

Stand upright with feet together. Push the palms out to both sides of the body with the fingertips upward and eyes looking straight ahead. Step forward with the left foot, and shift the body weight forward. Lift the right foot forward and kick it up to the left side of the head, then drop the right foot down to the inside of the left foot with eyes looking ahead. (Fig. 4-23)

Key Points: Straighten the supporting leg with the sole of the foot on the ground; straighten the oblique kick leg and kick it up to the opposite ear with the foot hooked; keep the upper body straight.

图 4-23　斜踢腿
Fig. 4-23 Oblique Kick

3. 侧踢腿   Side Kick

身体侧对正前方，并步站立。两掌向身体两侧插出，右掌指尖向右，左掌指尖向左；目视右侧。左脚经右脚前向右上步后，右脚勾起向上踢至右肩后方；同时，右掌收至左肩前，掌心向左，指尖向上，左掌上架至头上方，掌心向上；目视前方。（图4-24）

要点：左腿伸直，全脚掌着地；右腿伸直，勾脚经体侧踢向脑后，上体保持正直。

Stand upright with feet together with the side of body facing forward. Stretch out two palms to both sides of the body, with the fingertips of the right palm to the right and the fingertips of the left palm to the left, eyes looking to the right. After the left foot steps forward to the right through the front of the right foot, the right foot is raised and kicked up to the back of the right shoulder; at the same time, the right palm is retracted to the front of the left shoulder, with the palm to the left and the fingertips up; the left palm is placed above the head, with the palm up and eyes looking straight ahead. (Fig. 4-24)

Key Points: Straighten the left leg with the sole of the foot on the ground; straighten the right leg and kick the toes up to the back of the head through the side of the body, keeping the upper body upright.

图 4-24　侧踢腿
Fig. 4-24 Side Kick

4. 里合腿   Inward Swing Kick

　　并步站立。两掌向身体两侧推出，指尖向上；目视前方。重心前移，左脚向前上步，右脚勾起由右侧上踢，经面前向异侧做扇形摆动下落至左脚内侧；目视前方。（图4-25）

　　要点：支撑腿伸直，全脚掌着地；踢起腿脚内扣，上体保持正直。

Stand upright with feet together. Push the palms out to both sides of the body with the fingertips upward and eyes looking straight ahead. Move the center of gravity forward; step forward with the left foot; kick up the right leg to the right with the toes pointed inward, swing the leg to the left in a fan shape in front of the face and then put it down to the inside of the left foot; look straight ahead. (Fig. 4-25)

Key Points: Straighten the supporting leg with the sole of the foot on the ground; the toes of the kicking leg point inward and keep the upper body upright.

图 4-25　里合腿
Fig. 4-25 Inward Swing Kick

5. 外摆腿   Outward Swing Kick

并步站立。两掌向身体两侧推出，指尖向上；目视前方。重心前移，左脚向前上步，右脚勾起向左前、向上、向右划弧后下落至左脚内侧；目视前方。（图4-26）

要点：支撑腿伸直，全脚掌着地；上摆迅速，上体保持正直。

Stand upright with feet together. Push the palms out to both sides of the body with the fingertips upward and eyes looking straight ahead. Shift the center of gravity forward, step forward with the left foot, and kick up the right leg to draw an arc with the toes pointed inward. Swing the leg from the left front, upward, to the right, and then drop it to the inside of the left foot, with eyes looking ahead. (Fig. 4-26)

Key Points: Straighten the supporting leg with the sole of the foot on the ground; keep the upward swing fast and the upper body straight.

图 4-26　外摆腿
Fig. 4-26 Outward Swing Kick

6. 后撩腿 {Back Kick}

并步站立。两腿屈膝半蹲，同时，两臂后摆；随即左腿支撑，右脚向后上方撩踢。（图4-27）

要点：上体展身后仰，左腿伸直，右腿发力上撩。

Stand upright with feet together. Bend the knees to form a half squat; at the same time, swing both arms backward. Then supported by the left leg, kick the heel of the right leg towards the upper rear. (Fig. 4-27)

Key Points: Extend the upper body and lean backward, straighten the left leg, and kick the right leg forcibly up.

图 4-27 后撩腿
Fig. 4-27 Back Kick

7. 弹腿　　　　　　　　　　　　　　　　　　　　　　　Spring Kick

并步站立。重心前移，左脚向前上步；同时，两掌变拳上提至两腰间，拳心向上；随即右腿屈膝提起，小腿向前弹踢，弹直与腰平；目视前方。（图4-28）

要点：支撑腿伸直或稍屈，弹腿由屈至伸弹出，高不过腰，脚面绷平，力达脚尖。

Stand upright with feet together. Move the center of gravity forward, and step forward with the left foot; at the same time, turn the palms into fists and raise them to the waist, with the heart of fist facing upwards; then uplift the right leg with the knee bent, kick the calf forward forcefully to the height of the waist, with the knee straightened and eyes looking straight ahead. (Fig. 4-28)

Key Points: Straighten or slightly bend the supporting leg. The kicking leg pops out from bent to full extension, no higher than the waist, with the back of foot straightened and the force reaching the toes.

图 4-28　弹腿
Fig. 4-28　Spring Kick

8. 蹬腿   Heel Push Kick

并步站立。重心前移，左脚向前上步；同时，两掌变拳上提至两腰侧，拳心向上；随即右腿屈膝提起，脚尖勾起向前蹬出，脚尖向上；目视前方。（图4-29）

要点：支撑腿伸直或稍屈，蹬腿由屈至伸，脚尖勾起向前蹬出，高不过胸，低不过腰，力达脚跟。

Stand upright with feet together. Move the center of gravity forward, and step forward with the left foot; at the same time, turn the palms into fists and raise them to the waist, with the heart of fist facing upwards; then uplift the right leg with the knee bent, kick up the heel forward with the toes pointed upward and eyes looking ahead. (Fig. 4-29)

Key Points: Straighten or slightly bend the supporting leg, turn the kicking leg from bent to full extension, and kick up the heel forward with the toes pointed to the the height, no higher than the chest, no lower than the waist, and the force reaching the heel.

图 4-29 蹬腿
Fig. 4-29 Heel Push Kick

9. 侧踹腿 — Side Kick

并步站立。右脚经左脚前盖步，脚尖外展，随即两腿交叉屈膝半蹲；同时，两掌上摆至体前交叉，指尖向上；目视左方。右腿支撑站立，上体右倾，左腿屈膝，勾脚提起，随即向左侧踹腿，脚外侧向上；同时，两臂向两侧撑掌，指尖向前；目视左脚。（图4-30）

要点：支撑腿伸直，踹腿由屈至伸，脚尖勾起内扣向同侧踹出，力达脚跟。

Stand upright with feet together. Step forward with the right foot through the front of the left foot, spread the toes out, and then cross the legs and bend the knees to form a half squat; at the same time, swing the palms up to the front of the body, bend the elbows across, with the fingertips pointing upwards and eyes looking to the left. Stand on the right leg, lean the upper body to the right, lift the left leg with the knee bent and toes hooked, then thrust out the leg to the left side, with the outside of the foot upward; at the same time, extend the arms to both sides of the body, with the palms held up, the fingertips forward, and eyes looking at the left foot. (Fig. 4-30)

Key Points: Straighten the supporting leg, turn the kicking leg from bent to full extension, and strike it out to the same side with the toes pointed inward and the force reaching the heel.

图 4-30　侧踹腿
Fig. 4-30 Side Kick

10. 单拍脚   Single Foot Slap

　　并步站立。左脚向前上步，脚尖向前；同时两掌向前、向上至头前上方击掌，左掌心拍击右掌背，两掌心向前；目视前方。重心前移，左腿支撑，右腿向前、向上踢起，脚面绷平；同时，右掌心拍击右脚面；目视右掌。（图4-31）

　　要点：击响脚面，脚面绷平，踢摆、击响迅速；上下肢动作配合协调一致。

Stand upright with feet together. Step forward with the left foot and the toes face forward; at the same time, throw your palms forward and upward to the top of the head, and then slap the back of the right palm with the left palm, with both palms facing forward and eyes looking straight ahead. Move the center of gravity forward; supported by the left leg, kick up the right leg forward with the back of foot straightened; at the same time, the right palm slaps the right sole, with eyes looking at the right palm. (Fig. 4-31)

Key Points: When slapping the foot, straighten the back of foot and keep the kicking, swinging, and slapping quick. Keep the upper and lower body movements coordinated.

图 4-31　单拍脚
Fig. 4-31 Single Foot Slap

11. 里合腿击响 　　　　　　　　　　　　　　　　Inside Foot Slap

　　并步站立。两掌向身体两侧推出，指尖向上；目视前方。重心前移，左脚向前上步，右脚勾起由右侧上踢，经面前向异侧做扇形摆动时，左掌心合击右脚掌后，右脚下落至左脚内侧；目视前方。（图4-32）

　　要点：支撑腿伸直，全脚掌着地；合击快速。

Stand upright with feet together. Push the palms out to both sides of the body with the fingertips upward and eyes looking straight ahead. Move the center of gravity forward. Step forward with the left foot, and kick the right leg upward from the right side, with the toes pointed inward. When making a fan-shaped swing in front of your face to the opposite side, the left palm slaps the right sole, and then the right foot drops to the inside of the left foot, eyes looking straight ahead. (Fig. 4-32)

Key Points: Straighten the supporting leg with the sole of the foot on the ground and the slap should be fast.

图 4-32　里合腿击响
Fig. 4-32　Inside Foot Slap

12. 外摆腿击响　　　　　　　　　　　　　　　Outward Swing Slap

　　并步站立。两掌向身体两侧推出，指尖向上；目视前方。重心前移，左脚向前上步，右脚勾起向左前、向上、向右划弧时，两掌依次击拍右脚脚面后右脚下落至左脚内侧；目视前方。（图4-33）

　　要点：支撑腿伸直，全脚掌着地；击拍迅速，上体保持正直。

Stand upright with feet together. Push the palms out to both sides of the body with the fingertips upward and eyes looking straight ahead. Move the center of gravity forward. Step forward with the left foot, draw an arc with the toes of the right foot hooked, and swing the leg from the left front, upward, to the right. Then two palms successively slap the instep of the right foot, and the right foot drops to the inside of the left foot with eyes looking ahead. (Fig. 4-33)

Key Points: Straighten the supporting leg with the sole of the foot on the ground; keep the slap fast and the upper body straight.

图 4-33　外摆腿击响
Fig. 4-33 Outward Swing Slap

13. 后扫腿   Back Sweep

左脚在前成左弓步；两掌向前推出，掌心向前，指尖向上；目视前方。上体俯身右转，左腿屈膝全蹲成右仆步，同时，两掌撑扶至右腿下方地面；随即左脚跟提起，以前脚掌为轴，上体随右腿向右后扫转一周，右脚脚掌擦地。（图4-34）

要点：支撑腿全蹲，前脚掌为轴；扫转腿伸直，脚尖内扣，脚掌擦地，向右后方扫转一周。

Form the left bow stance with the left foot forward; push both palms forward with the center of palm forward, fingertips upward, and eyes looking straight ahead. Bend the upper body forward and turn it to the right; bend the left knee and squat to make a right crouching stance; at the same time, the two palms support the ground below the right leg. Then lift the left heel; taking the left forefoot as the axis, sweep the right leg and drive the upper body to the right rear in a circle, with the sole of the right foot rubbing the ground. (Fig. 4-34)

Key Points: Make a full squat with the supporting leg, taking the forefoot as the axis; straighten the sweeping leg with the toes pointed inward and the sole rubbing the ground and sweep the right leg backward in a circle.

图 4-34 后扫腿
Fig. 4-34 Back Sweep

14. 前扫腿   Front Sweep

两腿屈膝半蹲，左脚跟提起；右掌平举于身体右侧，指尖向上；左掌附于右臂内侧，指尖向上；目视右方。左脚向左开步，屈膝全蹲，以前脚掌为轴，右腿伸直，脚尖内扣，脚掌擦地向前扫转一周。（图4-35）

要点：支撑腿屈膝全蹲；扫转腿伸直，脚尖内扣，脚掌擦地。

Bend the knees to form a half squat with the left heel raised; raise the right palm horizontally to the right side of the body with fingertips pointing upward; attach the left palm to the inside of the right arm with fingertips pointing upward and eyes looking to the right. Step to the left with the left foot, bend the left knee to form a full squat, and take the forefoot as the axis; straighten the right leg with the toes pointed inward and sweep it forward in a circle with the sole of the leg rubbing the ground. (Fig. 4-35)

Key Points: Bend the knee of the supporting leg to form a full squat, with the forefoot as the axis; straighten the sweeping leg with the toes pointed inward and the sole rubbing the ground.

图 4-35　前扫腿
Fig. 4-35 Front Sweep

五、步 法   Footwork

1.上步   Stepping Forward

两脚前后错步站立。重心前移，右脚向左脚前上步，脚尖向前；目视
前方。（图4-36）

要点：上体正直，上步时脚跟先着地并依次过渡到全脚掌。

Stand with the feet crossed in front-and-back ways. Move the center of gravity
forward, and step forward with the right foot to the front of the left foot, toes forward
and eyes looking straight ahead. (Fig. 4-36)

Key Points: Keep the upper body upright. When you take a step forward, the heel
touches the ground first and then the full sole of the foot gradually falls on the ground.

图 4-36　上步
Fig. 4-36 Stepping Forward

2. 退步　　　　　　　　　　　　　　　　　　　　　　　Stepping Backward

两脚前后错步站立。重心后移，右脚向左脚后方退步，脚尖向前；目视前方。（图4-37）

要点：上体正直，退步时前脚掌先着地并依次过渡到全脚掌。

Stand with the feet crossed in front-and-back ways. Move the center of gravity backward, step backward with the right foot to the rear of left foot, toes forward and eyes looking straight ahead. (Fig. 4-37)

Key Points: Keep the upper body upright. When stepping backward, the forefoot touches the ground first and then the full sole of the foot gradually falls on the ground.

图 4-37　退步
Fig. 4-37 Stepping Backward

3. 开步　　　　　　　　　　　　　　　　　　　　　　　　Opening Stance

并步站立。右脚向右侧开步，脚尖向前；目视前方。（图4-38）

要点：开步时重心移至两腿之间，两脚平行站立。

Stand upright with feet together. Step to the right with the right foot, toes forward and eyes looking ahead. (Fig. 4-38）

Key Points: When making an opening stance, move the center of gravity between two legs, standing with feet paralleled.

图 4-38　开步
Fig. 4-38 Opening Stance

4. 并步 　　　　　　　　　　　　　　　　　　　　Folding Stance

并步站立。左脚向左开步，右脚继续向左一步，与左脚内侧并拢，重心落于两腿之间；目视前方。（图4-39）

要点：两脚脚尖向前，重心落于两腿之间。

Stand upright with feet together. Step to the left with the left foot, and then take another step to the left with the right foot, close to the inside of the left foot, with the center of gravity falling between two legs and eyes looking straight ahead. (Fig. 4-39)

Key Points: The toes of both feet point forward and the center of gravity is set between two legs.

图 4-39　并步
Fig. 4-39 Folding Stance

5. 跃步   Leaping Step

　　并步站立。左脚向前上步，脚尖向前；重心前移，右腿屈膝抬起，左脚蹬地向上跳起腾空，右脚、左脚依次向前落地。（图4-40）

　　要点：跳起腾空，落地轻灵。

Stand upright with feet together. Step forward with the left foot, toes forward; move the center of gravity forward, raise the right leg up with the knee bent, leap into the air with a drive on the left foot, and then land forward on the ground with the right foot and left foot in sequence. (Fig. 4-40)

Key Points: Jump up into the air and land lightly and agilely.

图 4-40　跃步
Fig. 4-40 Leaping Step

6. 插步   Back Cross Stance

　　并步站立。右腿屈膝抬起经左脚跟向左后方插步，前脚掌着地，右膝伸直，左腿微屈；同时，两掌变拳上提至两腰间，拳心向上；目视前方。（图4-41）

　　要点：上体正直，插步时前脚掌着地。

Stand upright with feet together. Lift the right leg up with the knee bent. Take a back cross stance to the left rear through the left heel, with the forefoot on the ground, the right knee straightened, and the left leg slightly bent; at the same time, turn the two palms into fists and raise them up to the waist with the heart of fist facing upward and eyes looking straight ahead. (Fig. 4-41)

Key Points: Keep the upper body upright and the forefoot on the ground when making the back cross stance.

图 4-41　插步
Fig. 4-41 Back Cross Stance

7. 弧形步   Curved Step

并步站立。两腿屈膝微蹲，随即左脚向左前方弧形上步，脚尖微外摆，右脚跟离地；目视前方。右脚经左脚内侧继续向左前方弧形上步，脚尖微内扣，左脚跟离地；左、右脚依次继续向前上步，直至半圆弧型走完；目视前方。（图4-42）

要点：上体正直，摆脚、扣脚依次进行，始终向着半圆弧方向。

Stand upright with feet together. Squat slightly with both knees bent, then step forward to the left front in an arc with the left foot, with the toes slightly turned outward, the right heel off the ground, and eyes looking straight ahead. The right foot keeps advancing to the left front in an arc through the inner side of the left foot, with the toes slightly pointed inward and the left heel off the ground; the left and right foot keep stepping forward one by one until the semi-circular arc is completed; look straight ahead. (Fig. 4-42)

Key Points: Keep the upper body upright. Step forward with the toes outward in an arch way and then advance forward with the toe-in step successively, always in the direction of the semi-circular arc.

图 4-42 弧形步
Fig. 4-42 Curved Step

8. 垫步　　　　　　　　　　　　　　　　　　Skipping Step

两脚前后错步站立。右脚向前上步，脚尖向前，左腿屈膝提起，右脚蹬地腾空向上跳起，右脚随即落地，左脚继续向前落地；目视前方。（图4-43）

要点：蹬地起跳脚与落地脚均为同一脚。

Stand with the feet crossed in front-and-back ways. Step forward with the right foot, toes forward; lift your left leg with the knee bent; leap into the air with a drive on the right foot; then immediately land on your right foot and continue to land on your left foot forward. Look straight ahead. (Fig. 4-43)

Key Points: The leaping foot and the landing foot are the same foot.

图 4-43　垫步
Fig. 4-43　Skipping Step

9. 击步 Hitting Step

并步站立。左脚向前上步后蹬地跳起腾空，右脚离地在空中碰击左脚内侧；右脚、左脚依次向前落地。（图4-44）

要点：两脚内侧碰击，两膝伸直。

Stand upright with feet together. The left foot steps forward and stamps on the ground to jump up into the air; the right foot hits the inside of the left foot in the air, and then the right foot and the left foot land forward in turn. (Fig. 4-44)

Key Points: Hit the inside of the feet and straighten the knees.

图 4-44　击步
Fig. 4-44 Hitting Step

六、平　衡 {Balance Techniques}

1. 提膝平衡 {Knee-raised Balance}

并步站立。右腿支撑站立，左腿屈膝提起。（图4-45）

要点：支撑腿直立站稳，提膝腿屈膝高抬过腰，小腿斜垂内扣，脚面绷平内收。

Stand upright with feet together. Stand on your right leg, and lift your left leg with the knee bent. (Fig. 4-45)

Key Points: Stand steadily upright with the supporting leg, and lift the knee-raised leg over the height of the waist, with the knee bent, the lower leg slanted inward, and the back of foot straightened inward.

图 4-45　提膝平衡
Fig. 4-45 Knee-raised Balance

2. 扣腿平衡   Back Cross-legged Balance

并步站立。右腿屈膝半蹲，左腿抬起，左脚勾脚贴扣至右膝后部。（图4-46）

要点：右腿半蹲，左脚背紧扣于右腿的后膝窝处。

Stand upright with feet together. Bend the right leg to form a half squat, lift the left leg with toes curved, and cling the left foot onto the back of the right knee. (Fig. 4-46)

Key Points: Form a half squat with the right leg and cling the back of the left foot firmly behind the right knee.

图 4-46　扣腿平衡
Fig. 4-46 Back Cross-legged Balance

3. 燕势平衡　　　　　　　　　　　　　　　　　　　Swallow Balance

并步站立。两腿屈膝半蹲，左脚跟提起；同时，两掌向前、向上摆至胸前交叉，右掌在外，左掌在内，指尖均向上；目视两掌。上体前俯，右腿支撑站立，左脚向后、向上举起，脚面绷平；同时，两掌内旋向两侧推出，指尖均向前，与肩同高；目视前方。（图4-47）

要点：后举腿伸直，高于水平位，躯干前俯略高于水平位，挺胸展腹。

Stand upright with feet together. Bend both knees to form a half squat with the left heel lifted; at the same time, swing both palms forward and upward until they are crossed in front of the chest, the right palm outside and the left palm inside, the fingertips pointing upward and eyes looking at both palms. Bend the upper body forward, stand on the right leg, and lift the left foot backward and upward with the back of foot straightened; at the same time, rotate both palms inward and push them out to both sides of the body, with fingertips facing forward at the height of the shoulders and eyes looking straight ahead. (Fig. 4-47)

Key Points: Straighten the back-lifted leg, higher than the horizontal level; bend the trunk forward, slightly higher than the horizontal level, chest out and abdomen stretched.

图 4-47　燕势平衡
Fig. 4-47 Swallow Balance

4. 侧身平衡 　　　　　　　　　　　　　　　Sideway Balance

　　并步站立。右腿屈膝半蹲，左腿屈膝，前脚掌着地；同时，右掌上提至右腰间，掌心向上；左掌体前下按，掌心向下；目视左掌。上体侧倾，重心移至右腿，右脚支撑站立，左脚向后上方举起，脚面绷平；同时，右掌向前下方插出，左掌向后上方插出；目视右掌。（图4-48）

　　要点：后举腿伸直高于水平位，躯干侧倾呈水平位。

Stand upright with feet together. Bend the right knee to form a half squat and bend the left knee with the forefoot on the ground; at the same time, lift the right palm to the waist with the palm facing upward; press the left palm downward in front of the body with the palm facing down, eyes looking at the left palm. Tilt the upper body with the center of gravity shifting onto the right leg; stand on the right foot and lift the left foot to the upper rear with the back of foot straightened; at the same time, thrust the right palm towards the lower front and the left palm towards the upper rear, eyes looking at the right palm. (Fig. 4-48)

Key Points: Straighten the back-lifted leg and raise it up to the side of the body, higher than the horizontal level; tilt the torso to the horizontal level.

图 4-48　侧身平衡
Fig. 4-48 Sideway Balance

5. 探海平衡　　　　　　　　　　　　　　　　　　Sea-searching Balance

并步站立。右腿屈膝半蹲，左腿屈膝，前脚掌着地；同时，右掌上提至右腰间，掌心向上；左掌体前下按，掌心向下；目视左掌。上体侧身前俯，重心移至右腿，右脚支撑站立，左脚向后上方举起，脚面绷平；同时，右掌向前下方插出，左掌向后上方插出；目视右掌。（图4-49）

要点：后举腿伸直高于水平位，躯干前倾略低于水平位，挺胸抬头。

Stand upright with feet together. Bend the right knee to form a half squat and bend the left knee with the forefoot on the ground; at the same time, lift the right palm to the waist with the palm facing upward; press the left palm downward in front of the body with the palm facing down, eyes looking at the left palm. Lean the upper body forward to one side, shifting the center of gravity onto the right leg; stand on the right foot and lift the left foot towards the upper rear with the back of foot straightened; at the same time, thrust the right palm towards the lower front and the left palm towards the upper rear, eyes looking at the right palm. (Fig. 4-49)

Key Points: Straighten the back-lifted leg and raise it up above horizontal level; slightly lean the torso forward below horizontal level, chest out and head up.

图 4-49　探海平衡
Fig. 4-49 Sea-searching Balance

6.仰身平衡   Backward-bending Balance

并步站立。右腿支撑站立，左腿屈膝提起；随即上体后仰，左腿向前举起，脚面绷平。（图4-50）

要点：支撑腿伸直或稍屈站稳，举起腿高于水平位，躯干后仰接近水平位。

Stand upright with feet together. Stand on the right leg, lift your left leg with the knee bent; then lean the upper body backward, lift the left leg forward with the back of foot straightened. (Fig. 4-50)

Key Points: Stand firmly with the supporting leg straight or slightly bent, raise the other leg higher than the horizontal level, and lean the torso backward close to the horizontal level.

图 4-50　仰身平衡
Fig. 4-50 Backward-bending Balance

7. 卧鱼平衡　　　　　　　　　　　　　　　　　　Fish-lying Balance

并步站立。右腿支撑站立，左腿小腿向后、向上屈收抬起，脚面绷平，脚底斜向上，躯干前俯斜倾；同时，左掌上架至头上方，掌心向上，右掌向右后方挑起；目视右后方。（图4-51）

要点：支撑腿伸直或稍屈站稳，后举腿大腿高于水平位，躯干斜倾接近水平位，挺胸、拧腰、展腹。

Stand upright with feet together. Stand on the right leg, bend the left calf and lift it backward and upward with the back of foot straightened, the sole of the foot slantly pointing upward, and the torso leaned forward; at the same time, hold the left palm above the head with the palm facing upward, the right palm raised to the right rear, and eyes looking to the right rear. (Fig. 4-51)

Key Points: Stand firmly with the supporting leg straight or slightly bent; raise the back-lifted leg higher than the horizontal level; lean the torse close to horizontal level, chest out, waist twisted, and abdomen stretched.

图 4-51　卧鱼平衡
Fig. 4-51 Fish-lying Balance

8. 盘腿平衡   Forward Crossed-legged Balance

并步站立。右腿屈膝半蹲，左腿屈膝，左脚踝关节盘放在右腿大腿上。（图4-52）

要点：右腿半蹲，左膝外展。

Stand upright with feet together. Bend the right knee to form a half squat, bend the left knee and extend it outward, and place the left ankle joint on the right thigh. (Fig. 4-52)

Key Points: Form a half squat with the right leg and extend the left knee outward.

图 4-52　盘腿平衡
Fig. 4-52 Forward Crossed-legged Balance

9. 望月平衡   Moon-watching Balance

并步站立。右腿支撑站立，左腿小腿向后、向上屈收抬起，脚面绷平，躯干侧倾向支撑腿同侧方向拧腰上翻；同时，左掌上架至头上方，掌心向上，右掌向右后方挑起；目视右侧。（图4-53）

要点：躯干侧倾向支撑腿同侧方向拧腰上翻，挺胸塌腰。

Stand upright with feet together. Stand on the right leg, bend the left calf and lift it backward and upward with the back of foot straightened, the sole of the foot pointed upward, and the torso leaned sideways to the same side of the supporting leg, with the waist twisted and the torso turned up; at the same time, place the left palm above the head with the palm facing upward and the right palm raised to the right rear, eyes looking to the right rear. (Fig. 4-53)

Key Points: The torso leans sideways to the same side of the supporting leg, with the waist twisted and the torso turned up. Remember to make the chest out and the waist down.

图 4-53　望月平衡
Fig. 4-53 Moon-watching Balance

七、跳 跃　　　　　　　　Jumping Techniques

1. 腾空飞脚　　　　　　　　Flying Front Kick

并步站立。右脚向前上步，脚尖外展，左脚向前上步；同时，两掌上摆胸前交叉。右脚抬起，左脚蹬地起跳，右脚在空中碰击左脚；随即右脚落地，左脚向前落步；右掌下落摆至身体右侧，指尖向右，略高于肩，左掌下落摆至身体左侧，指尖向左，与肩同高；目视左掌。右脚向前上步，蹬地向上跳起腾空，左腿屈膝提起；同时，右臂向下、向前、向上抡臂一周至头前上方，左掌摆至头前上方，左掌心拍击右掌背；随即右脚向前上方弹踢，右掌心拍击右脚面；右脚、左脚依次落地；目视前方。（图4-54）

要点：击响腿脚尖过肩，左腿提膝收于腹前；空中立身击掌，拍脚迅速准确。

Stand upright with feet together. Step forward with the right foot, toes outstretched, and then step forward with the left foot; at the same time, swing both palms up and make them crossed in front of the chest. Lift the right foot and leap into the air with a drive of the left foot, striking the left foot with the right foot in the air. Then the right foot lands on the ground and the left foot falls forward; the right palm falls and swings to the right side of the body, with fingertips to the right, slightly over the height of the shoulder; the left palm falls and swings to the left side of the body, with fingertips to the left, at the height of the shoulder, eyes looking at the left palm. Step forward with the right foot and leap into the air with a drive of the foot. Lift the left leg with the knee bent. At the same time, swing the right arm from downward, forward, and upward to the top of the head, swing the left palm overhead, and slap the back of the right palm with the left palm; then kick the right foot towards the upper front, slap the instep of the right foot with the right palm, and land on the ground in turn with the right foot and the left foot, eyes looking straight ahead. (Fig. 4-54)

Key Points: The toes of the slapping leg go above the shoulder, and lift the left knee up, close to the front of the abdomen; keep the body upright and clap the palms in the air; slap the foot quickly and accurately.

图 4-54　腾空飞脚
Fig. 4-54 Flying Front Kick

2. 旋风脚 Tornado Kick

并步站立。左脚向前上步，脚尖微外展，随后右脚向前屈膝扣脚上步；同时，两臂上摆至右上方；目视前方。重心右移，右脚蹬地跳起左转，左腿随体转向左摆腿，右腿向左上方踢起经面前里合，左拳变掌于面前迎击右脚前脚掌；身体向左后旋转360°。（图4-55）

要点：空中身体中正，脚高度过肩，击拍准确。

Stand upright with feet together. Step forward with the left foot, toes slightly outstretched; then bend the right knee forward and advance with a toe-in step; at the same time, swing the arms to the upper right with eyes looking straight ahead. Move the center of gravity to the right, stamp the right foot to jump up and turn left, swing the left leg as the body turns to the left, kick up the right leg to the upper left in front of your face, then swing it inward, and slap the right sole with the left palm in front of the face, rotating the body 360° to the left rear. (Fig. 4-55)

Key Points: Keep the body upright in the air, the height of the slapping leg over the shoulder, and the slapping accurate.

图 4-55 旋风脚
Fig. 4-55 Tornado Kick

3. 腾空外摆莲   Jump and Outward Swing Kick

并步站立。左脚向前上步，脚尖略内扣；同时，右臂前摆，左掌摆至体后；随即右脚向右弧形上步，脚尖微外展，右脚蹬地向上跳起腾空，左腿向上摆起，右腿向左上摆起经面前向右外摆；两臂上摆至头上方，左、右掌依次拍击右脚面；目视右脚。（图4-56）

要点：腾空摆腿幅度大，脚尖高度过肩，击拍准确。

Stand upright with feet together. Step forward with the left foot, toes slightly turned inward; at the same time, swing the right arm forward and swing the left palm to the back of the body; then step forward to the right in an arc with the right foot, toes slightly outstretched; stamp the right foot to jump up into the air. Swing the left leg upward, swing the right leg towards the upper left, and swing it outward to the right in front of your face; swing the arms up to the top of the head, and slap the right foot with the left palm and right palm in turn, eyes looking at the right foot. (Fig. 4-56)

Key Points: When you jump and swing the leg in the air, keep the range of the swinging motion large, swing your tiptoes over the height of your shoulder, and slap accurately.

图 4-56 腾空外摆莲
Fig. 4-56 Jump and Outward Swing Kick

4. 旋子   Butterfly Kick

并步站立。左脚向前上步，脚尖微外展；两臂上摆至身体两侧，掌心均向下；随即右脚向左前方上步，脚尖内扣，身体继续左转180°，两臂随转体继续平摆；目视前方。身体左转90°；左脚向右后方撤步，前脚掌着地，重心移至右腿，右腿屈膝；随即上体向左后拧转前俯，左脚蹬地腾空，右脚向后上方摆起，左腿随之摆起；两臂随腾空向后平摆；头上仰，目视前方。（图4-57）

要点：起跳、转身、提髋，空中腿伸直展体，塌腰、仰头。

Stand upright with feet together. Step forward with the left foot, toes slightly outstretched; swing both arms up to the sides of the body, palms down; then step towards the left front with the right foot, toes pointed inward, and the body turns 180° to the left; as the body spins, arms swing horizontally and eyes look straight ahead. Turn the body 90° to the left; step backwards to the right rear with the left foot, the forefoot on the ground, and the center of gravity shifts to the right leg, with the right knee bent; then twist the upper body to the left rear and bend it forward; stamp the left foot and jump into the air. As the right foot swings towards the upper rear, the left leg swings upwards; both arms swing horizontally towards the left rear in the air, with the head raised upward and eyes looking straight ahead. (Fig. 4-57)

Key Points: Jump up, turn around, and raise the hips. Straighten the legs in the air with the body stretched, the waist dropped and the head raised upward.

图 4-57 旋子
Fig. 4-57 Butterfly Kick

5. 侧空翻   Aerial Cartwheel

并步站立。右脚向前上步，左腿屈膝提起后，右脚蹬地跳起向前垫步，右脚落地，左脚依次向前落步，随即上体前屈，左脚蹬地，右腿、左腿依次向后、向上、向前摆动，两腿在空中分开（在空中做向左侧空翻动作），随即右脚、左脚依次落地；目视右下方。（图4-58）

要点：上体前屈后再蹬地。

Stand upright with feet together. Step forward with the right foot. After you lift your left leg with the knee bent, stamp the ground with your right foot to skip forward. When the right foot lands, the left foot lands successively forward, and then the upper body bends forward. Stamp the ground with your left foot, swing the right leg and left leg backward, upward, and forward in turn, separate the two legs in the air (make a left cartwheel in the air), and then land on the ground with the right foot and left foot in turn. Look to the lower right. (Fig. 4-58)

Key Points: Bend the upper body forward and then kick off the ground.

图 4-58 侧空翻
Fig. 4-58 Aerial Cartwheel

八、跌扑滚翻 Tumbling Techniques

1. 跌竖叉 Falling Front Split

并步站立。两腿屈膝下蹲蹬地跳起，随即左脚向前蹬出，脚尖向上，大腿后侧着地；右脚向后铲出，腿部内侧贴地，脚掌着地，脚尖向右。（图4-59）

要点：两腿同时落地，两膝伸直，上体微前倾。

Stand upright with feet together. Bend the two knees to squat down and jump up with the drive of two feet; then kick the left foot forward, toes up and the back of the thigh on the ground. Kick the right foot backward, with the inside of the leg on the ground, the sole of the foot on the ground, and toes to the right. (Fig. 4-59)

Key Points: Both legs land on the ground at the same time, with knees straightened and the upper body leaned forward slightly.

图 4-59 跌竖叉
Fig. 4-59 Falling Front Split

2. 侧摔　　　　　　　　　　　　　　　　　　　　　Side Fall

并步站立。身体后仰并向右倾，左腿支撑，右腿向前挺膝前伸；同时，右臂向前、向上摆至体后，左掌收于右臂内侧；目视右掌。上体继续向右倾，随即着地，右腿外侧着地，右臂内侧着地，左手着地；目视右掌。（图4-60）

要点：身体各部位同时着地。

Stand upright with feet together. Lean your body backward and towards the right. Supported by the left leg, straighten and stretch the right leg; at the same time, swing the right arm forward and upward to the back of the body, with the left palm retracted into the inside of the right arm, eyes looking at the right palm. Keep leaning the upper body to the right, then fall onto the ground with the outside of the right leg, the inside of the right arm, and the left hand; look to the right. (Fig. 4-60)

Key Points: All parts of the body touch the ground at the same time.

图 4-60　侧摔
Fig. 4-60　Side Fall

3. 抢背 — Shoulder Roll

并步站立。左脚上步屈膝，上体随之前倾；随即右脚离地，左掌向前下撑扶地面，右掌落于左掌后方横向撑扶地面。左脚蹬地，右腿向上摆起；同时，低头弓身，右肩、背部依次着地，团身前滚后立起。（图4-61）

要点：抢背落地时，肩后部、背部、臀部、大腿后侧依次着地；身体团身前滚。

Stand upright with feet together. The left foot steps forward with the knee bent, and the upper body leans forward accordingly; then as the right foot leaves off the ground, the left palm forwardly supports on the ground and the right palm falls behind the left palm to support on the ground horizontally. Stamp on the ground with the left foot and swing the right leg upward; at the same time, bow your body with the head down, roll forward with the body tucked, the right shoulder and the back successively touch the ground, and stand up then. (Fig. 4-61)

Key Points: When landing after the shoulder roll, the back of the shoulders, the back, the buttocks, and the back of the thighs land on the ground in sequence. Roll forward with the body tucked.

图 4-61　抢背
Fig. 4-61 Shoulder Roll

4.鲤鱼打挺   Carp's Leap

身体仰卧。两腿向上举起，两膝伸直；同时，两掌扶按两大腿，指尖相对；臀部离地，两脚继续向后摆至与上肢靠拢；随即两脚向上、向前快速摆动使身体腾空，两脚同时落地，身体向上立起；目视前方。（图4-62）

要点：两腿摆动快速，顶髋、挺腹、挺胸。

Lie on your back. Lift your legs up and straighten your knees; at the same time, press two thighs with both palms, with the fingertips facing each other; lift the buttocks off the ground, and continue swinging the feet backward until they are close to the upper limbs; then as both feet quickly swing upward and forward, leap your body into the air like the carp, and land on the ground with both feet at the same time; stand up; look straight ahead. (Fig. 4-62)

Key Points: Swing the legs quickly and keep the hips out, the abdomen out and the chest out.

图 4-62　鲤鱼打挺
Fig. 4-62 Carp's Leap

5.盘腿跌   Crossed-legged Drop

并步站立。左脚向前上步后右脚向前屈膝扣脚上步，同时，两臂上摆至身体右上方；随即身体向右侧倾斜，重心移至右腿，右脚蹬地向上跳起腾空，左腿屈膝抬起；上体左转，右腿向右、向上经脸前摆至左侧。上体左侧着地，左膝弯曲，左腿外侧着地，右腿伸直，右大腿内侧贴靠左大

腿内侧，右脚掌着地；同时，两肘弯曲，左前臂内侧着地，两掌着地；目视右方。（图4-63）

要点：左腿弯曲摆动，右腿立圆摆动；身体各部位同时着地。

Stand upright with feet together. After stepping forward with the left foot, step forward with the right foot, the knee bent and toes pointed inward. At the same time, swing the arms up to the upper right of the body. Then lean the body to the right, shift the center of gravity to the right leg, leap into the air with a drive of the right foot, and raise the left leg up with the knee bent. Turn the upper body to the left, swing the right leg from the right, upward, to the left in front of the face. The left side of the upper body falls on the ground with the left knee bent, the outside of the left leg on the ground, the right leg straightened, the inside of the right thigh close to the inside of the left thigh, and the right sole on the ground. At the same time, bend both elbows, and the inside of the left forearm and both palms land on the ground with eyes looking to the right. (Fig. 4-63)

Key Points: The left leg swings curvedly, and the right leg swings in a vertical circle; all parts of the body fall on the ground at the same time.

图 4-63　盘腿跌
Fig. 4-63 Crossed-legged Drop

长拳段前九级
考评技术内容

A Nine-tier Pre-Duan Grading
System for Chang Quan

长拳段前一级   Chang Quan: Pre-Duan Level 1

长拳段前一级
Chang Quan:
Pre-Duan
Level 1

技术内容

① 招数：5个动作。

② 拳法：2种（冲拳、劈拳）。

③ 手型：1种（拳）。

④ 步型：1种（马步）。

Technical Contents

① Move: 5 moves.

② Fist Technique: 2 fists (punching fist, chopping fist).

③ Hand Form: 1 hand form (fist).

④ Stance: 1 stance (horse stance).

练习长拳段前一级开始前行抱拳礼。

Before your practice, perform the palm-fist salute.

1. 预备势   Preparatory Posture

要点： 头正颈直，下颌微收，挺胸收腹。（图5-1）

Key Points: Keep the head upright and the neck straight, the chin slightly drew inward, the chest out and the abdomen in. (Fig. 5-1)

图 5-1　预备势
Fig. 5-1 Preparatory Posture

2. 并步抱拳   Hold Fists with Feet Together

要点：挺胸立腰，两肘后夹，两拳紧贴腰侧，拳心向上。（图5-2）

Key Points: Keep the chest high and the waist erected, elbows tucked backward, two fists close to the waist and the heart of fist pointing upward. (Fig. 5-2)

图 5-2　并步抱拳
Fig. 5-2　Hold Fists with Feet Together

3. 马步冲拳   Punch Fist in a Horse Stance

要点：冲拳力达拳面，马步时大腿呈水平位，上下肢动作协调一致。（图5-3）

Key Points: The punching force should reach the face of fist, the thighs are at horizontal level in the horse stance, and the movements of the upper and lower limbs are coordinated. (Fig. 5-3)

图 5-3　马步冲拳
Fig. 5-3　Punch Fist in a Horse Stance

4. 马步劈拳   Chop Fist in a Horse Stance

要点：劈拳力达拳轮。（图5-4）

Key Points: The chopping force should reach the fist curve. (Fig. 5-4)

图 5-4　马步劈拳
Fig. 5-4　Chop Fist in a Horse Stance

5. 收势   Closing Posture

要点：头正颈直，挺胸收腹，两肘后夹，两拳紧贴腰侧，拳心向上。
（图5-5）

Key Points: Keep the head upright and the neck straight, the chest high and the abdomen in, elbows tucked backward, two fists close to the waist and the heart of fist pointing upward. (Fig. 5-5)

图 5-5　收势
Fig. 5-5　Closing Posture

练习长拳段前一级结束后行抱拳礼。

At the end of your practice, perform the palm-fist salute.

长拳段前二级 Chang Quan: Pre-Duan Level 2

长拳段前二级
Chang Quan:
Pre-Duan
Level 2

技术内容

① 招数：6个动作。

② 掌法：2种（推掌、亮掌）。

③ 手型：2种（拳、掌）。

④ 步型：2种（马步、弓步）。

Technical Contents

① Move: 6 moves.

② Palm Technique: 2 palms (pushing palm, showing palm).

③ Hand Form: 2 hand forms (fist, palm).

④ Stance: 2 stances (horse stance, bow stance).

练习长拳段前二级开始前行抱拳礼。

Before your practice, perform the palm-fist salute.

1. 预备势   Preparatory Posture

要点：头正颈直，下颌微收，挺胸收腹。（图5-6）

Key Points: Keep the head upright and the neck straight, the chin slightly drew inward, the chest out and the abdomen in. (Fig. 5-6)

图 5-6　预备势
Fig. 5-6　Preparatory Posture

2. 并步抱拳　　　　　　　　　　　　Hold Fists with Feet Together

要点：挺胸立腰，两肘后夹，两拳紧贴腰侧，拳心向上。（图5-7）

Key Points: Keep the chest high and the waist erected, elbows tucked backward, two fists close to the waist and the heart of fist pointing upward. (Fig. 5-7)

图 5-7　并步抱拳
Fig. 5-7 Hold Fists with Feet Together

3. 马步推掌　　　　　　　　　　　　Push Palm in a Horse Stance

要点：推掌迅速有力，力达小指外沿。（图5-8）

Key Points: Push the palm quickly and powerfully with the force reaching the outer edge of the little finger. (Fig. 5-8)

图 5-8　马步推掌
Fig. 5-8 Push Palm in a Horse Stance

4. 弓步推掌 Push Palm in a Bow Stance

要点：右脚蹬地成左弓步，左膝与脚面垂直，大腿呈水平位；右腿蹬直，脚尖内扣；推掌力达掌外沿；转身推掌与弓步动作协调一致。（图5-9）

Key Points: Form a left bow stance with a drive of the right foot, the left knee perpendicular to the instep and the thigh at horizontal level; straighten the right leg with the toes pointed inward; push the palm with the force reaching the outer edge of the palm; keep the body turning, palm pushing and bow stance well coordinated. (Fig. 5-9)

图 5-9 弓步推掌
Fig. 5-9 Push Palm in a Bow Stance

5. 马步亮掌 Show Palm in a Horse Stance

要点：左掌摆至头顶上方抖腕亮掌，右掌收至左肩前；马步时两膝外撑，大腿呈水平位，上下肢动作配合协调一致。（图5-10）

Key Points: Swing the left palm to the top of the head, shake the wrist and show the palm. Retract the right palm to the front of the left shoulder. When making the horse stance, knees are outwardly supported, the thighs are at horizontal level, and the movements of the upper and lower limbs are coordinated. (Fig. 5-10)

图 5-10 马步亮掌
Fig. 5-10 Show Palm in a Horse Stance

6. 收势   Closing Posture

要点：头正颈直，挺胸收腹，两肘后夹，两拳紧贴腰侧，拳心向上。（图5-11）

Key Points: Keep the head upright and the neck straight, the chest high and the abdomen in, elbows tucked backward, two fists close to the waist and the heart of fist pointing upward. (Fig. 5-11)

图 5-11　收势
Fig. 5-11 Closing Posture

练习长拳段前二级结束后行抱拳礼。

At the end of your practice, perform the palm-fist salute.

长拳段前三级   Chang Quan: Pre-Duan Level 3

长拳段前三级
Chang Quan:
Pre-Duan
Level 3

技术内容

① 招数：6个动作。

② 拳法：1种（冲拳）。

③ 掌法：3种（架掌、摆掌、推掌）。

④ 手型：3种（拳、掌、勾）。

⑤ 步型：2种（弓步、仆步）。

Technical Contents

① Move: 6 moves.

② Fist Technique: 1 fist (punching fist).

③ Palm Technique: 3 palms (upholding palm, swing palm, pushing palm).

④ Hand Form: 3 hand forms (fist, palm, hook).

⑤ Stance: 2 stances (bow stance, crouching stance).

练习长拳段前三级开始前行抱拳礼。

Before your practice, perform the palm-fist salute.

1. 预备势 Preparatory Posture

要点：头正颈直，下颌微收，挺胸收腹。（图5-12）

Key Points: Keep the head upright and the neck straight, the chin slightly drew inward, the chest out and the abdomen in. (Fig. 5-12)

2. 并步抱拳 Hold Fists with Feet Together

要点：挺胸立腰，两肘后夹，两拳紧贴腰侧，拳心向上。（图5-13）

Key Points: Keep the chest high and the waist erected, elbows tucked backward, two fists close to the waist and the heart of fist pointing upward. (Fig. 5-13)

图 5-12 预备势
Fig. 5-12 Preparatory Posture

图 5-13 并步抱拳
Fig. 5-13 Hold Fists with Feet Together

3. 弓步架掌冲拳　　　　　Bow Stance with Palm Upholding and Fist Punching

要点：左脚向左上步成左弓步，膝与脚面垂直，大腿呈水平位，右腿蹬直，脚尖内扣；右掌架至头顶上方，左拳向左冲出，力达拳面。（图5-14）

Key Points: Step forward with the left foot to form a left bow stance; the knee is perpendicular to the instep, with the thigh at horizontal level, and the right leg is straightened with the toes pointed inward. Hold the right palm up to the top of the head, punch the left fist to the left, with the force reaching the face of fist. (Fig. 5-14)

4. 仆步摆掌　　　　　　　　Swing Palm in a Crouching Stance

要点：左掌摆至右肩前；仆步时挺胸、立腰，左腿平铺伸直；仆步与摆掌动作协调一致。（图5-15）

Key Points: Swing the left palm to the front of the right shoulder; when you are in the crouching stance, keep the chest out, the waist up, and the left leg horizontally straightened; make the crouching stance and the palm swinging coordinated. (Fig. 5-15)

图 5-14　弓步架掌冲拳
Fig. 5-14 Bow Stance with Palm Upholding and Fist Punching

图 5-15　仆步摆掌
Fig. 5-15 Swing Palm in a Crouching Stance

5. 弓步勾手推掌   Bow Stance with Hook Hand and Palm Pushing

要点：重心前移，右脚蹬地成左弓步，右脚内扣，右膝蹬直；推掌力达掌外沿。（图5-16）

Key Points: Move the center of gravity forward and form a left bow stance with a drive of the right foot; point the right toes inward, straighten the right knee, and make the pushing force reach the outer edge of the palm. (Fig. 5-16)

图 5-16 弓步勾手推掌
Fig. 5-16 Bow Stance with Hook Hand and Palm Pushing

6. 收势   Closing Posture

要点：头正颈直，挺胸收腹，两肘后夹，两拳紧贴腰侧，拳心向上。（图5-17）

Key Points: Keep the head upright and the neck straight, the chest high and the abdomen in, elbows tucked backward, two fists close to the waist and the heart of fist pointing upward. (Fig. 5-17)

图 5-17 收势
Fig. 5-17 Closing Posture

练习长拳段前三级结束后行抱拳礼。

At the end of your practice, perform the palm-fist salute.

长拳段前四级   Chang Quan: Pre-Duan Level 4

长拳段前四级
Chang Quan:
Pre-Duan
Level 4

技术内容

① 招数：7个动作。

② 拳法：3种（劈拳、冲拳、砸拳）。

③ 掌法：1种（亮掌）。

④ 手型：3种（拳、掌、勾）。

⑤ 步型：4种（马步、弓步、歇步、仆步）。

Technical Contents

① Move: 7 moves.

② Fist Technique: 3 fists (chopping fist, punching fist, hammer striking fist).

③ Palm Technique: 1 palm (showing palm).

④ Hand Form: 3 hand forms (fist, palm, hook).

⑤ Stance: 4 stances (horse stance, bow stance, resting stance, crouching stance).

练习长拳段前四级开始前行抱拳礼。

Before your practice, perform the palm-fist salute.

1.预备势   Preparatory Posture

要点：头正颈直，下颌微收，挺胸收腹。（图5-18）

Key Points: Keep the head upright and the neck straight, the chin slightly drew inward, the chest out and the abdomen in. (Fig. 5-18)

2.并步抱拳   Hold Fists with Feet Together

要点：挺胸立腰，两肘后夹，两拳紧贴腰侧，拳心向上。（图5-19）

Key Points: Keep the chest high and the waist erected, elbows tucked backward, two fists close to the waist and the heart of fist pointing upward. (Fig. 5-19)

图 5-18 预备势
Fig. 5-18 Preparatory Posture

图 5-19 并步抱拳
Fig. 5-19 Hold Fists with Feet Together

3. 马步劈拳   Chop Fist in a Horse Stance

要点：挺胸、塌腰，两肩松沉；劈拳力达拳轮，动作协调一致。（图 5-20）

Key Points: Keep the chest out, the waist down, and the shoulders dropped and relaxed; the chopping force reaches the curve of fist and the movements are coordinated. (Fig. 5-20)

图 5-20 马步劈拳
Fig. 5-20 Chop Fist in a Horse Stance

4. 弓步冲拳   Punch Fist in a Bow Stance

要点：动作转换快速，冲拳力达拳面。（图5-21）

Key Points: Quickly switch the movements with the punching force reaching the face of fist. (Fig. 5-21)

图 5-21 弓步冲拳
Fig. 5-21 Punch Fist in a Bow Stance

5. 歇步砸拳   Strike Fist in a Resting Stance

要点：立圆抡臂下砸，力达拳背；两腿交叉全蹲，动作连贯，完成迅速。（图5-22）

Key Points: Swing the arms in a vertical circle, and then strike them down, with the force reaching the back of fists; cross both legs and squat, making the cross-legged crouching stance with coherent movements and fast completion. (Fig. 5-22)

图 5-22　歇步砸拳
Fig. 5-22 Strike Fist in a Resting Stance

6. 仆步勾手亮掌　　Crouching Stance with Hook Hand and Palm Showing

要点：左掌摆至头顶上方，抖腕亮掌，右掌变勾手摆至体后，指尖向上；仆步时挺胸、立腰，右腿平铺伸直，脚尖内扣；屈蹲腿全蹲。（图5-23）

Key Points: Swing the left palm above the head, shake the wrist and show the palm. Turn the right palm into a hook hand and swing it to the back of the body, with the fingertips pointing upward. When making the crouching stance, keep the chest out, the waist erected, and the right leg horizontally straightened with toes turned inward. The squatting leg should be fully squatted. (Fig. 5-23)

图 5-23　仆步勾手亮掌
Fig. 5-23 Crouching Stance with Hook Hand and Palm Showing

7.收势 Closing Posture

要点：头正颈直，挺胸收腹，两肘后夹，两拳紧贴腰侧，拳心向上。
（图5-24）

Key Points: Keep the head upright and the neck straight, the chest high and the abdomen in, elbows tucked backward, two fists close to the waist and the heart of fist pointing upward. (Fig. 5-24)

图 5-24 收势
Fig. 5-24 Closing Posture

练习长拳段前四级结束后行抱拳礼。

At the end of your practice, perform the palm-fist salute.

长拳段前五级　　Chang Quan: Pre-Duan Level 5

长拳段前五级
Chang Quan:
Pre-Duan
Level 5

技术内容

① 招数：8个动作。

② 拳法：3种（冲拳、架拳、栽拳）。

③ 掌法：2种（摆掌、亮掌）。

④ 肘法：1种（格肘）。

⑤ 手型：3种（拳、掌、勾）。

⑥ 步型：5种（马步、弓步、仆步、歇步、虚步）。

Technical Contents

① Move: 8 moves.

② Fist Technique: 3 fists (punching fist, upholding fist, plunging fist).

③ Palm Technique: 2 palms (swing palm, showing palm).

④ Elbow Technique: 1 elbow (blocking elbow).

⑤ Hand Form: 3 hand forms (fist, palm, hook).

⑥ Stance: 5 stances (horse stance, bow stance, crouching stance, resting stance, empty stance).

练习长拳段前五级开始前行抱拳礼。

Before your practice, perform the palm-fist salute.

1. 预备势　　　　　　　　　　　　　　　　　Preparatory Posture

要点：头正颈直，下颌微收，挺胸收腹。（图5-25）

Key Points: Keep the head upright and the neck straight, the chin slightly drew inward, the chest out and the abdomen in. (Fig. 5-25)

图 5-25　预备势
Fig. 5-25　Preparatory Posture

2. 并步抱拳 — Hold Fists with Feet Together

要点：挺胸立腰，两肘后夹，两拳紧贴腰侧，拳心向上。（图5-26）

Key Points: Keep the chest high and the waist erected, elbows tucked backward, two fists close to the waist and the heart of fist pointing upward. (Fig. 5-26)

图 5-26　并步抱拳
Fig. 5-26 Hold Fists with Feet Together

3. 马步格挡 — Shove Aside in a Horse Stance

要点：格挡力达前臂，马步时两膝外撑，大腿呈水平位。（图5-27）

Key Points: When shoving aside, the force reaches the forearm of the blocking elbow; when making the horse stance, two knees are outwardly supported with the thighs at horizontal level. (Fig. 5-27)

图 5-27　马步格挡
Fig. 5-27 Shove Aside in a Horse Stance

4. 弓步冲拳   Punch Fist in a Bow Stance

要点：冲拳力达拳面，成弓步时后膝伸直，弓步与冲拳动作协调一致。（图5-28）

Key Points: The punching force reaches the face of fist. Straighten the back knee in a bow stance and make the bow stance and the punching coordinated. (Fig. 5-28)

图 5-28 弓步冲拳

Fig. 5-28 Punch Fist in a Bow Stance

5. 仆步摆掌   Swing Palm in a Crouching Stance

要点：左掌摆至右肩前，成仆步时挺胸、立腰，左腿平铺伸直；仆步与摆掌动作协调一致。（图5-29）

Key Points: Swing the left palm to the front of the right shoulder; during the crouching stance, keep the chest out, the waist up, and the left leg horizontally straightened; make the crouching stance and the palm swinging coordinated. (Fig. 5-29)

图 5-29 仆步摆掌

Fig. 5-29 Swing Palm in a Crouching Stance

6. 歇步勾手亮掌　　　　　Resting Stance with Hook Hand and Palm Showing

要点： 歇步时两腿交叉屈膝全蹲，左脚全脚掌着地，脚尖外展，右脚脚跟离地；臀部坐于右腿小腿上。（图5-30）

Key Points: When making a resting stance, cross both legs with knees bent to form a full squat, with the sole of the left foot on the ground; with toes outstretched, the right heel is off the ground and the buttocks sit on the right calf. (Fig. 5-30)

图 5-30　歇步勾手亮掌
Fig. 5-30 Resting Stance with Hook Hand and Palm Showing

7. 虚步架栽拳　　　　　　Empty Stance with Fist Downward and Arm Uplifting

要点：成虚步时重心落于左腿，右腿微屈，脚尖点地；上架拳、下栽拳完成迅速。（图5-31）

Key Points: When making an empty stance, the center of gravity falls onto the left leg, with the right leg slightly bent and the toes touching the ground; complete the upholding fist and plunging fist quickly. (Fig. 5-31)

8. 收势　　　　　　　　　　　　　　　Closing Posture

要点：头正颈直，挺胸收腹，两肘后夹，两拳紧贴腰侧，拳心向上。（图5-32）

Key Points: Keep the head upright and the neck straight, the chest high and the abdomen in, elbows tucked backward, two fists close to the waist and the heart of fist pointing upward. (Fig. 5-32)

图 5-31　虚步架栽拳
Fig. 5-31 Empty Stance with Fist Downward and Arm Uplifting

图 5-32　收势
Fig. 5-32 Closing Posture

练习长拳段前五级结束后行抱拳礼。

At the end of your practice, perform the palm-fist salute.

长拳段前六级 　　　Chang Quan: Pre-Duan Level 6

长拳段前六级
Chang Quan:
Pre-Duan
Level 6

技术内容

① 招数：11个动作。

② 拳法：5种（架拳、栽拳、冲拳、砸拳、劈拳）。

③ 掌法：2种（架掌、挑掌）。

④ 肘法：1种（盘肘）。

⑤ 手型：3种（拳、掌、勾）。

⑥ 步型：5种（虚步、弓步、马步、歇步、仆步）。

⑦ 腿法：1种（正踢腿）。

Technical Contents

① Move: 11 moves.

② Fist Technique: 5 fists (upholding fist, plunging fist, punching fist, hammer striking fist, chopping fist).

③ Palm Technique: 2 palms (upholding palm, uplifting palm).

④ Elbow Technique: 1 elbow (hook elbow).

⑤ Hand Form: 3 hand forms (fist, palm, hook).

⑥ Stance: 5 stances (empty stance, bow stance, horse stance, resting stance, crouching stance).

⑦ Leg Technique: 1 leg (front kick).

练习长拳段前六级开始前行抱拳礼。

Before your practice, perform the palm-fist salute.

1. 预备势   Preparatory Posture

要点：头正颈直，下颌微收，挺胸收腹。（图5-33）

Key Points: Keep the head upright and the neck straight, the chin slightly drew inward, the chest out and the abdomen in. (Fig. 5-33)

2. 并步抱拳   Hold Fists with Feet Together

要点：挺胸立腰，两肘后夹，两拳紧贴腰侧，拳心向上。（图5-34）

Key Points: Keep the chest high and the waist erected, elbows tucked backward, two fists close to the waist and the heart of fist pointing upward. (Fig. 5-34)

图 5-33　预备势
Fig. 5-33 Preparatory Posture

图 5-34　并步抱拳
Fig. 5-34 Hold Fists with Feet Together

3. 虚步架栽拳   Empty Stance with Fist Downward and Arm Uplifting

要点：成虚步时重心落于右腿，左腿微屈，脚尖点地；上架拳、下栽拳完成迅速。（图5-35）

Key Points: When making an empty stance, the center of gravity falls onto the right leg, with the left leg slightly bent and the toes touching the ground; complete the upholding fist and plunging fist quickly. (Fig. 5-35)

图 5-35　虚步架栽拳
Fig. 5-35 Empty Stance with Fist Downward and Arm Uplifting

4. 弓步冲拳   Punch Fist in a Bow Stance

要点：右冲拳力达拳面；左膝与脚面垂直，大腿呈水平位；右膝伸直，脚尖内扣；两脚全脚掌着地。（图5-36）

Key Points: The force of the right punching reaches the face of fist; the left knee is perpendicular to the instep and the thigh is at horizontal level; straighten the right knee with the toes pointed inward; the soles of both feet are on the ground. (Fig. 5-36)

图 5-36　弓步冲拳
Fig. 5-36 Punch Fist in a Bow Stance

5. 马步冲拳   Punch Fist in a Horse Stance

要点：马步与冲拳同时完成，动作迅速。（图5-37）

Key Points: Complete the horse stance and fist punching at the same time with quick movements. (Fig. 5-37)

图 5-37　马步冲拳
Fig. 5-37 Punch Fist in a Horse Stance

6. 并步砸拳   Strike Fist with Feet Together

要点：拳由上向下随屈臂下砸，拳心向上，力达拳背。（图5-38）

Key Points: Pound the fist down from the top with the arm bent, the heart of fist facing upward, and the force reaching the back of fist. (Fig. 5-38)

图 5-38　并步砸拳
Fig. 5-38 Strike Fist with Feet Together

7. 正踢腿   Front Kick

要点：支撑腿伸直，全脚掌着地；踢起腿伸直、勾脚踢触及前额，上体保持正直。（图5-39）

Key Points: Straighten the supporting leg with the sole of the foot on the ground; straighten the kicking leg and kick it up with toes pointed until it touches the forehead, keeping the upper body straight. (Fig. 5-39)

图 5-39　正踢腿
Fig. 5-39 Front Kick

8. 马步盘肘   Hook Elbow in a Horse Stance

要点：盘肘快速有力，前臂由外向内盘肘，力达前臂，上臂与前臂挟紧。（图5-40）

Key Points: Form the hook elbow quickly and forcefully. When moving the forearm from an outward to an inward position to form the hook elbow, the force reaches the forearm, and the upper arm and the forearm are held tightly together. (Fig. 5-40)

图 5-40　马步盘肘
Fig. 5-40 Hook Elbow in a Horse Stance

9. 歇步勾手挑掌　　　　Resting Stance with Hook Hand and Palm Uplifting

要点：臂由下向上翘腕立掌上挑，力达四指。（图5-41）

Key Points: Lift the arm upward and press the wrist downward to erect the palm, with the force reaching four fingers. (Fig. 5-41)

图 5-41　歇步勾手挑掌
Fig. 5-41 Resting Stance with Hook Hand and Palm Uplifting

10. 仆步劈拳　　　　　　　　　Chop Fist in a Crouching Stance

要点：劈拳力达拳轮，仆步时平铺腿伸直，脚尖内扣；屈蹲腿全蹲。（图5-42）

Key Points: The chopping force reaches the fist curve; when making the crouching stance, straighten the stretching leg with toes turned inward; form a full squat with the squatting leg. (Fig. 5-42)

图 5-42　仆步劈拳
Fig. 5-42 Chop Fist in a Crouching Stance

11. 收势   Closing Posture

要点：头正颈直，挺胸收腹，两肘后夹，两拳紧贴腰侧，拳心向上。

（图5-43）

Key Points: Keep the head upright and the neck straight, the chest high and the abdomen in, elbows tucked backward, two fists close to the waist and the heart of fist pointing upward. (Fig. 5-43)

图 5-43　收势
Fig. 5-43 Closing Posture

练习长拳段前六级结束后行抱拳礼。

At the end of your practice, perform the palm-fist salute.

长拳段前七级 — Chang Quan: Pre-Duan Level 7

长拳段前七级
Chang Quan:
Pre-Duan
Level 7

技术内容

① 招数：13个动作。

② 拳法：1种（冲拳）。

③ 掌法：4种（推掌、架掌、摆掌、亮掌）。

④ 肘法：2种（格肘、压肘）。

⑤ 手型：3种（拳、掌、勾）。

⑥ 步型：5种（马步、弓步、仆步、歇步、虚步）。

⑦ 腿法：2种（弹腿、蹬腿）。

Technical Contents

① Move: 13 moves.

② Fist Technique: 1 fist (punching fist).

③ Palm Technique: 4 palms (pushing palm, upholding palm, swying palm, showing palm).

④ Elbow Technique: 2 elbows (blocking elbow, pressing elbow).

⑤ Hand Form: 3 hand forms (fist, palm, hook).

⑥ Stance: 5 stances (horse stance, bow stance, crouching stance, resting stance, empty stance).

⑦ Leg Technique: 2 legs (spring kick, heel push kick).

练习长拳段前七级开始前行抱拳礼。

Before your practice, perform the palm-fist salute.

1. 预备势   Preparatory Posture

要点：头正颈直，下颌微收，挺胸收腹。（图5-44）

Key Points: Keep the head upright and the neck straight, the chin slightly drew inward, the chest out and the abdomen in. (Fig. 5-44)

2. 并步抱拳   Hold Fists with Feet Together

要点：挺胸立腰，两肘后夹，两拳紧贴腰侧，拳心向上。（图5-45）

Key Points: Keep the chest high and the waist erected, elbows tucked backward, two fists close to the waist and the heart of fist pointing upward. (Fig. 5-45)

图 5-44　预备势
Fig. 5-44 Preparatory Posture

图 5-45　并步抱拳
Fig. 5-45 Hold Fists with Feet Together

3. 马步格肘   Block Elbow in a Horse Stance

要点：马步时两膝外撑，大腿呈水平位。（图5-46）

Key Points: When making the horse stance, both knees are outwardly supported and the thighs are at horizontal level. (Fig. 5-46)

图 5-46　马步格肘

Fig. 5-46 Block Elbow in a Horse Stance

4. 弓步冲拳   Punch Fist in a Bow Stance

要点：右冲拳力达拳面，左弓步时膝与脚面垂直，大腿呈水平位，右腿蹬直，脚尖内扣。（图5-47）

Key Points: The force of the right punching reaches the face of fist. When making the left bow stance, the knee is perpendicular to the instep, with the thigh at horizontal level. The right leg is straightened with the toes pointed inward. (Fig. 5-47)

图 5-47　弓步冲拳

Fig. 5-47 Punch Fist in a Bow Stance

5. 弹腿冲拳　　　　　　　　　　　　　　　Spring Kick and Punch Fist

要点：弹腿由屈至伸弹出，脚面绷平，高与腰平，力达脚尖；弹腿与冲拳动作协调一致。（图5-48）

Key Points: When kicking the leg from bent to full extension, the back of foot should be straightened at the same height of the waist, with the force reaching the toes; keep the spring kick and fist punching coordinated. (Fig. 5-48)

图 5-48　弹腿冲拳
Fig. 5-48 Spring Kick and Punch Fist

6. 弓步推掌　　　　　　　　　　　　　　Push Palm in a Bow Stance

要点：右弓步时膝与脚面垂直，大腿呈水平位，左腿扣脚蹬直；推掌力达掌外沿。（图5-49）

Key Points: When making the right bow stance, the knee is perpendicular to the instep with the thigh at horizontal level, the left leg straightened and the toes pointed inward; the pushing force reaches the outer edge of the palm. (Fig. 5-49)

图 5-49　弓步推掌
Fig. 5-49 Push Palm in a Bow Stance

7. 蹬腿   Heel Push Kick

要点：支撑腿伸直或稍屈，蹬腿由屈至伸，脚尖勾起向前蹬出，高不过胸，低不过腰，力达脚跟。（图5-50）

Key Points: Straighten or slightly bend the supporting leg; turn the kicking leg from bent to full extension; kick it forward with the toes pointed upward, neither higher than the chest nor lower than the waist, with the force reaching the heel. (Fig. 5-50)

8. 弓步架推掌   Bow Stance with Palm Upholding and Pushing

要点：推掌时从腰间立掌向前推出，力达掌外沿。（图5-51）

Key Points: When pushing the palm, push it forward from the waist with the palm erected and the force reaching the outer edge of the palm. (Fig. 5-51)

图 5-50 蹬腿   图 5-51 弓步架推掌

Fig. 5-50 Heel Push Kick   Fig. 5-51 Bow Stance with Palm Upholding and Pushing

9. 仆步摆掌   Swing Palm in a Crouching Stance

要点：仆步时挺胸、立腰，平铺腿伸直；上下肢动作配合协调一致。（图5-52）

Key Points: When making the crouching stance, keep the chest out, the waist up, the stretching leg straightened, and the movements of the upper and lower body coordinated. (Fig. 5-52)

图 5-52 仆步摆掌
Fig. 5-52 Swing Palm in a Crouching Stance

10. 歇步勾手亮掌　　Resting Stance with Hook Hand and Palm Showing

要点：歇步时两腿交叉屈膝全蹲，左腿全脚掌着地，脚尖外展；右腿脚跟离地，臀部坐于右腿小腿上。（图5-53）

Key Points: When making a resting stance, cross both legs with knees bent to form a full squat, with the sole of the left foot on the ground and the toes outstretched; the right heel is off the ground and the buttocks sit on the right calf. (Fig. 5-53)

图 5-53 歇步勾手亮掌
Fig. 5-53 Resting Stance with Hook Hand and Palm Showing

11. 马步压肘 Press Elbow in a Horse Stance

要点：马步时两膝外撑，大腿呈水平位；压肘力达肘尖。（图5-54）

Key Points: When making the horse stance, knees are outwardly supported and the thighs are at horizontal level. The elbow pressing force reaches the tip of the elbow. (Fig. 5-54)

图 5-54　马步压肘
Fig. 5-54　Press Elbow in a Horse Stance

12. 虚步勾手推掌 Empty Stance with Hook Hand and Palm Pushing

要点：推掌力达掌外沿；虚步时重心落于右腿，大腿呈水平位。（图5-55）

Key Points: The pushing force reaches the outer edge of the palm; when making the empty stance, the center of gravity falls onto the right leg, with the thigh at horizontal level. (Fig. 5-55)

图 5-55　虚步勾手推掌
Fig. 5-55　Empty Stance with Hook Hand and Palm Pushing

13. 收势 Closing Posture

要点： 头正颈直，挺胸收腹，两肘后夹，两拳紧贴腰侧，拳心向上。
（图5-56）

Key Points: Keep the head upright and the neck straight, the chest high and the abdomen in, elbows tucked backward, two fists close to the waist and the heart of fist pointing upward. (Fig. 5-56)

图 5-56　收势
Fig. 5-56 Closing Posture

练习长拳段前七级结束后行抱拳礼。

At the end of your practice, perform the palm-fist salute.

长拳段前八级　　Chang Quan: Pre-Duan Level 8

技术内容

① 招数：15个动作。

② 拳法：2种（冲拳、架拳）。

③ 掌法：7种（劈掌、盖掌、穿掌、撩掌、推掌、亮掌、挑掌）。

④ 肘法：1种（盘肘）。

⑤ 手型：3种（拳、掌、勾）。

⑥ 步型：5种（弓步、马步、仆步、歇步、虚步）。

⑦ 腿法：2种（弹腿、正踢腿）。

⑧ 平衡：1种（提膝平衡）。

Technical Contents

① Move: 15 moves.

② Fist Technique: 2 fists (punching fist, upholding fist).

③ Palm Technique: 7 palms (hacking palm, downward pressing palm, thrusting palm, scooping palm, pushing palm, showing palm, uplifting palm).

④ Elbow Technique: 1 elbow (hook elbow).

⑤ Hand Form: 3 hand forms (fist, palm, hook).

⑥ Stance: 5 stances (bow stance, horse stance, crouching stance, resting stance, empty stance).

⑦ Leg Technique: 2 legs (spring kick, front kick).

⑧ Balances: 1 balance (knee-raised balance).

练习长拳段前八级开始前行抱拳礼。

Before your practice, perform the palm-fist salute.

1. 预备势   Preparatory Posture

要点：头正颈直，下颌微收，挺胸收腹。（图5-57）

Key Points: Keep the head upright and the neck straight, the chin slightly drew inward, the chest out and the abdomen in. (Fig. 5-57)

2. 并步抱拳   Hold Fists with Feet Together

要点：挺胸立腰，两肘后夹，两拳紧贴腰侧，拳心向上。（图5-58）

Key Points: Keep the chest high and the waist erected, elbows tucked backward, two fists close to the waist and the heart of fist pointing upward. (Fig. 5-58)

图 5-57　预备势　　　　　　　　图 5-58　并步抱拳
Fig. 5-57 Preparatory Posture　　Fig. 5-58 Hold Fists with Feet Together

3. 弓步冲拳　　　　　　　　　　　　　　　　Punch Fist in a Bow Stance

要点：弓步与冲拳动作协调一致，力达拳面，一前一后，两力相争。
（图5-59）

Key Points: The bow stance and the fist punching are coordinated, with the force reaching the face of fist; two forces struggle against each other, one in the front, the other back. (Fig. 5-59)

图 5-59　弓步冲拳
Fig. 5-59 Punch Fist in a Bow Stance

4. 提膝劈掌　　　　　　　　　　　　　　　　Uplift Knee and Hack Palm

要点：下劈掌由上向下呈立圆，动作开合舒展；右腿提膝迅速，左腿稳定。（图5-60）

Key Points: Hack the palm down from the top in a vertical circle, with movements graceful and expansive; lift the right knee quickly and keep the left leg stable. (Fig. 5-60)

图 5-60　提膝劈掌
Fig. 5-60 Uplift Knee and Hack Palm

5. 马步架冲拳　　　　Horse Stance with Fist Upholding and Punching

要点：动作连贯，力点准确顺达；马步与架冲拳同时完成。（图 5-61）

Key Points: The movements are coherent and the force points are accurate with smooth delivery; complete the horse stance and fist upholding and punching at the same time. (Fig. 5-61)

图 5-61　马步架冲拳
Fig. 5-61 Horse Stance with Fist Upholding and Punching

6. 提膝穿掌 Uplift Knee and Thrust Palm

要点： 退步盖掌，提膝挺胸立身，收膝快速敏捷，支撑稳定。（图 5-62）

Key Points: Step backward with the palm pressed downward; uplift the knee with the chest out and the body upright; retract the knee quickly and agilely; keep the support stable. (Fig. 5-62)

图 5-62 提膝穿掌
Fig. 5-62 Uplift Knee and Thrust Palm

7. 仆步穿掌 Thrust Palm in a Crouching Stance

要点： 右腿屈膝下蹲成左仆步，左掌沿左腿内侧向前穿出，仆步与穿掌动作配合一致。（图5-63）

Key Points: Bend the right knee and squat down to form a left crouching stance; thrust the left palm forward along the inner side of the left leg; keep the crouching stance and the palm piercing coordinated. (Fig. 5-63)

图 5-63 仆步穿掌
Fig. 5-63 Thrust Palm in a Crouching Stance

8. 弓步勾手撩掌　　　　　　Bow Stance with Hook Hand and Scoop Palm

要点：重心前移成左弓步，右掌直臂向前撩出，掌心向上，力达掌心。（图5-64）

Key Points: Move the center of gravity forward into a left bow stance; thrust the right palm forward with the right arm straight, the palm facing upward, and the force reaching the center of palm. (Fig. 5-64)

图 5-64　弓步勾手撩掌
Fig. 5-64 Bow Stance with Hook Hand and Scoop Palm

9. 弓步双推掌　　　　　　　　Push Double Palms in a Bow Stance

要点：双掌沉腕前推，两肘微屈，两肩向下松沉，力达掌外沿；上下肢动作配合协调一致。（图5-65）

Key Points: Push both palms forward with the wrists dropped, the elbows slightly bent, the shoulders relaxed and dropped, and the force reaching the outer edge of the palms; keep the upper and lower limbs well coordinated. (Fig. 5-65)

图 5-65　弓步双推掌
Fig. 5-65 Push Double Palms in a Bow Stance

10. 抱拳弹踢（右左）   Hold Fists and Spring Kick (right and left)

要点：两拳收抱至腰间；弹腿由屈至伸弹出，脚面绷平，高度与腰平，力达脚尖。（图5-66）

Key Points: Hold two fists to the waist; kick the leg from bent to full extension with the back of the foot straightened at the waist level, and the force reaching the toes. (Fig. 5-66)

图 5-66　抱拳弹踢（右左）
Fig. 5-66 Hold Fists and Spring Kick (right and left)

11. 正踢腿   Front Kick

要点：左掌上架至头顶上方；支撑腿接近伸直，全脚掌着地；踢起腿伸直，勾脚踢至触及前额，上体保持正直。（图5-67）

Key Points: Uphold the left palm above the head; straighten the supporting leg with the sole of the foot on the ground; straighten the kicking leg and kick it up with toes pointed until it touches the forehead; keep the upper body straight. (Fig. 5-67)

图 5-67　正踢腿
Fig. 5-67　Front Kick

12. 马步盘肘　　　　　　　　　　　　　　　Hook Elbow in a Horse Stance

　　要点：上体左转，右腿前落成马步；盘肘快速有力，前臂由外向内盘肘，力达前臂，上臂与前臂挟紧。（图5-68）

Key Points: Turn the upper body to the left; step forward with the right leg to form a horse stance. Form the hook elbow quickly and forcefully. When moving the forearm from the outside to the inside to form the hook elbow, the force reaches the forearm, and the upper arm and the forearm are held tightly together. (Fig. 5-68)

图 5-68　马步盘肘
Fig. 5-68　Hook Elbow in a Horse Stance

13. 歇步勾手亮掌　　　　Resting Stance with Hook Hand and Palm Showing

要点：左掌摆至头顶上方抖腕亮掌，右掌变勾手摆至体后，指尖向上；歇步时两腿交叉屈膝全蹲，臀部坐于左腿小腿上；上下肢动作配合协调一致。（图5-69）

Key Points: Swing the left palm above the head, shake the wrist and show the palm. Turn the right palm into a hook hand and swing it to the back of the body, with the fingertips pointing upward. When making a resting stance, cross both legs with knees bent to form a full squat, and the buttocks sit on the left calf; keep the movements of the upper and lower body coordinated. (Fig. 5-69)

图 5-69　歇步勾手亮掌
Fig. 5-69 Resting Stance with Hook Hand and Palm Showing

14. 虚步挑掌　　　　　　　　　　　Uplift Palm in an Empty Stance

要点：左掌体前沉腕上挑；虚步时重心落于右腿，大腿呈水平位；左腿微屈，脚尖点地；虚步与挑掌同时完成。（图5-70）

Key Points: Press the left wrist downward to erect the palm in front of the body; the center of gravity falls on the right leg in empty stance, with the thigh at horizontal level; slightly bend the left leg with toes on the ground; complete the empty stance and uplifting palm at the same time. (Fig. 5-70)

图 5-70　虚步挑掌
Fig. 5-70 Uplift Palm in an Empty Stance

15. 收势   Closing Posture

要点：头正颈直，挺胸收腹，两肘后夹，两拳紧贴腰侧，拳心向上。
（图5-71）

Key Points: Keep the head upright and the neck straight, the chest high and the abdomen in, elbows tucked backward, two fists close to the waist and the heart of fist pointing upward. (Fig. 5-71)

图 5-71　收势
Fig. 5-71 Closing Posture

练习长拳段前八级结束后行抱拳礼。

At the end of your practice, perform the palm-fist salute.

长拳段前九级 Chang Quan: Pre-Duan Level 9

长拳段前九级
Chang Quan:
Pre-Duan
Level 9

技术内容

① 招数：17个动作。

② 拳法：2种（冲拳、栽拳）。

③ 掌法：5种（亮掌、挑掌、穿掌、推掌、摆掌）。

④ 肘法：1种（盘肘）。

⑤ 手型：3种（拳、掌、勾）。

⑥ 步型：4种（弓步、马步、歇步、虚步）。

⑦ 腿法：3种（弹腿、侧踹腿、单拍脚）。

⑧ 步法：2种（跃步、插步）。

⑨ 平衡：1种（提膝平衡）。

Technical Contents

① Move: 17 moves.

② Fist Technique: 2 fists (punching fist, plunging fist).

③ Palm Technique: 5 palms (showing palm, uplifting palm, thrusting palm, pushing palm, swing palm).

④ Elbow Technique: 1 elbow (hook elbow).

⑤ Hand Form: 3 hand forms (fist, palm, hook).

⑥ Stance: 4 stances (bow stance, horse stance, resting stance, empty stance).

⑦ Leg Technique: 3 legs (spring kick, side kick, single foot slap).

⑧ Footwork: 2 footwork (leaping step, back cross stance).

⑨ Balance: 1 balance (knee-raised balance).

练习长拳段前九级开始前行抱拳礼。

Before your practice, perform the palm-fist salute.

1.预备势   Preparatory Posture

要点：头正颈直，下颌微收，挺胸收腹。（图5-72）

Key Points: Keep the head upright and the neck straight, the chin slightly drew inward, the chest out and the abdomen in. (Fig. 5-72)

2.并步抱拳   Hold Fists with Feet Together

要点：挺胸立腰，两肘后夹，两拳紧贴腰侧，拳心向上。（图5-73）

Key Points: Keep the chest high and the waist erected, elbows tucked backward, two fists close to the waist and the heart of fist pointing upward. (Fig. 5-73)

图 5-72　预备势
Fig. 5-72 Preparatory Posture

图 5-73　并步抱拳
Fig. 5-73 Hold Fists with Feet Together

3. 弓步冲拳   Punch Fist in a Bow Stance

要点：冲拳力达拳面，弓步时右腿绷直，弓步与冲拳动作协调一致。
（图5-74）

Key Points: The punching force reaches the face of fist; when making the bow stance, straighten the right leg and keep the bow stance and fist punching coordinated. (Fig. 5-74)

图 5-74　弓步冲拳
Fig. 5-74 Punch Fist in a Bow Stance

4. 弹腿冲拳   Spring Kick and Punch Fist

要点：左拳前冲，力达拳面；支撑腿伸直，弹腿由屈至伸向前弹出，高与腰平，力达脚尖。（图5-75）

Key Points: Punch the left fist forward with the force reaching the face of fist; straighten the supporting leg, kick the other leg forward from bent to full extension at the waist level with the force reaching the toes. (Fig. 5-75)

图 5-75　弹腿冲拳
Fig. 5-75 Spring Kick and Punch Fist

5. 马步盘肘   Hook Elbow in a Horse Stance

要点：盘肘快速有力，前臂由外向内盘肘，力达前臂，上臂与前臂挟紧。（图5-76）

Key Points: Form the hook elbow quickly and forcefully. When moving the forearm from an outward to an inward position to form the hook elbow, the force reaches the forearm, and the upper arm and the forearm are held tightly together. (Fig. 5-76)

6. 歇步勾手亮掌   Resting Stance with Hook Hand and Palm Showing

要点：左掌摆至头顶上方，抖腕亮掌，右掌变勾手摆至体后，指尖向上；歇步时两腿交叉屈膝全蹲，臀部坐于左腿小腿上；上下肢动作配合协调一致。（图5-77）

Key Points: Swing the left palm above the head, shake the wrist and show the palm. Turn the right palm into a hook hand and swing it to the back of the body, with the fingertips pointing upward. When making a resting stance, cross both legs with knees bent to form a full squat, and the buttocks sit on the left calf; keep the movements of the upper and lower body coordinated. (Fig. 5-77)

图 5-76　马步盘肘
Fig. 5-76　Hook Elbow in a Horse Stance

图 5-77　歇步勾手亮掌
Fig. 5-77　Resting Stance with Hook Hand and Palm Showing

7. 侧踹腿 — Side Kick

要点：支撑腿伸直，踹腿由屈至伸，脚尖勾起、内扣向同侧踹出，力达脚跟。（图5-78）

Key Points: Straighten the supporting leg, kick the uplifting leg from bent to full extension to the same side, with the toes pointed inward and the force reaching the heel. (Fig. 5-78)

图 5-78　侧踹腿
Fig. 5-78 Side Kick

8. 虚步挑掌 — Uplift Palm in an Empty Stance

要点：虚步时重心落于右腿，大腿呈水平位；左腿微屈，脚尖点地；虚步与挑掌同时完成。（图5-79）

Key Points: The center of gravity falls on the right leg in empty stance, with the thigh at horizontal level; slightly bend the left leg with toes on the ground; complete the empty stance and uplifting palm at the same time. (Fig. 5-79)

图 5-79　虚步挑掌

Fig. 5-79 Uplift Palm in an Empty Stance

9. 提膝上穿掌　　　　　　　　　　　Uplift Knee and Thrust Palm Upward

要点： 提膝挺胸立身，收膝快速敏捷；支撑稳定。（图5-80）

Key Points: Uplift the knee with the chest out and the body upright; retract the knee quickly and agilely; keep the support stable. (Fig. 5-80)

图 5-80　提膝上穿掌

Fig. 5-80 Uplift Knee and Thrust Palm Upward

10. 单拍脚（左右）   Single Foot Slap (left and right)

要点：踢摆迅速，击响准确；上下肢动作配合协调一致。（图5-81）

Key Points: Keep the kicking and swinging quick, the slapping accurate, and the upper and lower body movements coordinated. (Fig. 5-81)

图 5-81　单拍脚（左右）
Fig. 5-81 Single Foot Slap (left and right)

11. 大跃步前穿   Forward Giant Leap

要点：空中展身摆掌，跃步敏捷；上下肢动作配合协调一致。（图5-82）

Key Points: Extend the body and swing the palms in the air, leap agilely, and keep the upper and lower body movements coordinated. (Fig. 5-82)

图 5-82　大跃步前穿
Fig. 5-82 Forward Giant Leap

图 5-82　大跃步前穿（续）
Fig. 5-82 Forward Giant Leap (continued)

12. 弓步冲拳　　　　　　　　　　Punch Fist in a Bow Stance

要点：右冲拳力达拳面；左弓步时左膝与脚面垂直，大腿呈水平位，右腿扣脚蹬直。（图5-83）

Key Points: The force of the right punching reaches the face of fist. When making the left bow stance, the knee is perpendicular to the instep, with the thigh at horizontal level, the right leg straightened, and the toes pointed inward. (Fig. 5-83)

图 5-83　弓步冲拳
Fig. 5-83 Punch Fist in a Bow Stance

13. 弓步双推掌   Push Double Palms in a Bow Stance

要点：双掌沉腕推出，两肘微屈，两肩向下松沉，力达掌外沿；上下肢动作配合协调一致。（图5-84）

Key Points: Push both palms forward with the wrists dropped, the elbows slightly bent, the shoulders relaxed and dropped, and the force reaching the outer edge of the palms; keep the upper and lower limbs well coordinated. (Fig. 5-84)

图 5-84　弓步双推掌
Fig. 5-84 Push Double Palms in a Bow Stance

14. 插步双摆掌   Swing Double Palms in a Back Cross Stance

要点：立圆、抡臂、摆掌，后插步迅速；摆掌与后插步动作协调一致。（图5-85）

Key Points: Swing the arms in a vertical circle and sway the palms, swiftly make the back cross stance, and keep palm swaying and back cross stance well coordinated. (Fig. 5-85)

图 5-85　插步双摆掌
Fig. 5-85 Swing Double Palms in a Back Cross Stance

15. 弓步勾手推掌　　　　　Bow Stance with Hook Hand and Palm Pushing

要点：推掌力达掌外沿；左弓步时左膝与脚面垂直，大腿呈水平位，右腿扣脚蹬直。（图5-86）

Key Points: The pushing force reaches the outer edge of the palm; the left knee is perpendicular to the instep in left bow stance, with the thigh at horizontal level; straighten the right leg with the toes pointed inward. (Fig. 5-86)

图 5-86　弓步勾手推掌
Fig. 5-86 Bow Stance with Hook Hand and Palm Pushing

16. 虚步架栽拳　　　　Empty Stance with Fist Downward and Arm Uplifting

要点：虚步时重心落于右腿，大腿呈水平位，左腿微屈，脚尖点地；上架拳、下栽拳完成迅速。（图5-87）

Key Points: When making an empty stance, the center of gravity falls onto the right leg, with the thigh at horizontal level, the left leg slightly bent and the toes touching the ground; complete the upholding fist and plunging fist quickly. (Fig. 5-87)

图 5-87　虚步架栽拳
Fig. 5-87 Empty Stance with Fist Downward and Arm Uplifting

17. 收势   Closing Posture

要点：头正颈直，挺胸收腹，两肘后夹，两拳紧贴腰侧，拳心向上。（图5-88）

Key Points: Keep the head upright and the neck straight, the chest high and the abdomen in, elbows tucked backward, two fists close to the waist and the heart of fist pointing upward. (Fig. 5-88)

图 5-88　收势
Fig. 5-88　Closing Posture

练习长拳段前九级结束后行抱拳礼。

At the end of your practice, perform the palm-fist salute.

长拳段位
考评技术内容

Duanwei Grading System
for Chang Quan

一段长拳　　　　　　　　　　　Chang Quan: Grade 1

技术内容

① 招数：34式。

② 段数：4段。

③ 手型：3种（拳、掌、勾）。

④ 步型：3种（马步、弓步、虚步）。

⑤ 拳法：5种（劈拳、冲拳、架拳、栽拳、砸拳）。

⑥ 掌法：5种（推掌、砍掌、摆掌、撩掌、架掌）。

⑦ 腿法：2种（蹬腿、弹腿）。

Technical Contents

① Move: 34 moves.

② Section: 4 sections.

③ Hand Form: 3 hand froms (fist, palm, hook).

④ Stance: 3 stances (horse stance, bow stance, empty stance).

⑤ Fist Technique: 5 fists (chopping fist, punching fist, upholding fist, plunging fist, hammer striking fist).

⑥ Palm Technique: 5 palms (pushing palm, chopping palm, swing palm, scooping palm, upholding palm).

⑦ Leg Technique: 2 legs (heel push kick, spring kick).

动作名称

预备势

第一段

1. 起势

2. 马步双劈拳

3. 拗弓步冲拳

4. 蹬腿冲拳

5. 马步冲拳

6. 马步双劈拳

7. 拗弓步冲拳

8. 蹬腿冲拳

9. 马步冲拳

第二段

10. 弓步推掌

11. 拗弓步推掌

12. 弓步搂手砍掌

13. 弓步穿手推掌

14. 弓步推掌

15. 拗弓步推掌

16. 弓步搂手砍掌

17. 弓步穿手推掌

第三段

18. 虚步上架

19. 马步下压

20. 拗弓步冲拳

21. 马步冲拳

22. 虚步上架

23. 马步下压

24. 拗弓步冲拳

25. 马步冲拳

第四段

26. 弓步双摆掌

27. 弓步撩掌

28. 推掌弹踢

29. 弓步上架推掌

30. 弓步双摆掌

31. 弓步撩掌

32. 推掌弹踢

33. 弓步上架推掌

34. 收势

一段长拳
Chang Quan:
Grade 1

Names of the Movements

Preparatory Posture

Section 1

1. Starting Posture

2. Chop Double Fists in a Horse Stance

3. Punch Fist in a Bow Stance (the opposite side)

4. Heel Push Kick and Punch Fist

5. Punch Fist in a Horse Stance

6. Chop Double Fists in a Horse Stance

7. Punch Fist in a Bow Stance (the opposite side)

8. Heel Push Kick and Punch Fist

9. Punch Fist in a Horse Stance

Section 2

10. Push Palm in a Bow Stance

11. Push Palm in a Bow Stance (the opposite side)

12. Bow Stance with Hand Grabbing and Palm Chopping

13. Bow Stance with Arm Thrusting and Palm Pushing

14. Push Palm in a Bow Stance

15. Push Palm in a Bow Stance (the opposite side)

16. Bow Stance with Hand Grabbing and Palm Chopping

17. Bow Stance with Arm Thrusting and Palm Pushing

Section 3

18. Uphold Fist in an Empty Stance

19. Strike Arm Downward in a Horse Stance

20. Punch Fist in a Bow Stance (the opposite side)

21. Punch Fist in a Horse Stance

22. Uphold Fist in an Empty Stance

23. Strike Arm Downward in a Horse Stance

24. Punch Fist in a Bow Stance (the opposite side)

25. Punch Fist in a Horse Stance

Section 4

26. Swing Double Palms in a Bow Stance

27. Scoop Palm in a Bow Stance

28. Push Palm and Spring Kick

29. Bow Stance with Arm Upholding and Palm Pushing

30. Swing Double Palms in a Bow Stance

31. Scoop Palm in a Bow Stance

32. Push Palm and Spring Kick

33. Bow Stance with Arm Upholding and Palm Pushing

34. Closing Posture

练习一段长拳开始前行抱拳礼。

Before your practice, perform the palm-fist salute.

预备势 Preparatory Posture

要点：挺胸、收腹、立腰，头正颈直。（图6-1）

Key Points: Keep the chest out, the abdomen in, the waist up, the head upright and the neck straight. (Fig. 6-1)

图 6-1　预备势
Fig. 6-1 Preparatory Posture

第一段　Section 1

1. 起势   Starting Posture

要点：挺胸立腰，两肘后夹，两拳紧贴腰侧，拳心向上。（图6-2）

Key Points: Keep the chest high and the waist erected, two elbows tucked backward, two fists close to the waist and the heart of fist pointing upward. (Fig. 6-2)

图 6-2　起势
Fig. 6-2 Starting Posture

2. 马步双劈拳   Chop Double Fists in a Horse Stance

要点：挺胸，两肩松沉，劈拳力达拳轮，动作协调一致。（图6-3）

Key Points: Keep the chest out, the shoulders relaxed and dropped, with the chopping force reaching the fist curve and the movements coordinated. (Fig. 6-3)

图 6-3　马步双劈拳
Fig. 6-3 Chop Double Fists in a Horse Stance

3. 拗弓步冲拳　　　　　　　　Punch Fist in a Bow Stance (the opposite side)

要点：冲拳拳眼向上，力达拳面，成弓步时后膝蹬直。（图6-4）

Key Points: The eye of the punching fist faces upward, the force reaches the face of fist, and the back knee is straight in bow stance. (Fig. 6-4)

图 6-4　拗弓步冲拳
Fig. 6-4 Punch Fist in a Bow Stance (the opposite side)

4. 蹬腿冲拳　　　　　　　　　　　Heel Push Kick and Punch Fist

要点：蹬腿时由屈至伸，脚尖勾起蹬出，高不过胸，低不过腰，力达脚跟；冲拳力达拳面，动作协调一致。（图6-5）

Key Points: When kicking the leg, kick it out from bent to full extension with the toes pointed upward. The height is neither higher than the chest nor lower than the waist, with the force reaching the heel. The punching force reaches the face of fist and the movements are coordinated. (Fig. 6-5)

图 6-5　蹬腿冲拳
Fig. 6-5 Heel Push Kick and Punch Fist

5. 马步冲拳   Punch Fist in a Horse Stance

要点：转腰顺肩，冲拳快速有力。（图6-6）

Key Points: Turn the waist, extend the shoulder, and punch the fist fast and powerfully. (Fig. 6-6)

图 6-6　马步冲拳
Fig. 6-6 Punch Fist in a Horse Stance

6. 马步双劈拳   Chop Double Fists in a Horse Stance

要点：挺胸，两肩松沉，劈拳力达拳轮，动作协调一致。（图6-7）

Key Points: Keep the chest out, the shoulders relaxed and dropped, with the chopping force reaching the fist curve and the movements coordinated. (Fig. 6-7)

图 6-7　马步双劈拳
Fig. 6-7 Chop Double Fists in a Horse Stance

7. 拗弓步冲拳   Punch Fist in a Bow Stance (the opposite side)

要点： 冲拳拳眼向上，力达拳面，弓步后膝蹬直。（图6-8）

Key Points: The eye of the punching fist faces upward, the force reaches the face of fist, and the back knee is straight in bow stance. (Fig. 6-8)

图 6-8 拗弓步冲拳
Fig. 6-8 Punch Fist in a Bow Stance (the opposite side)

8. 蹬腿冲拳   Heel Push Kick and Punch Fist

要点： 蹬腿时由屈至伸，脚尖勾起蹬出，高不过胸，低不过腰，力达脚跟；冲拳力达拳面，动作协调一致。（图6-9）

Key Points: When kicking the leg, kick it out from bent to full extension with the toes pointed upward. The height is neither higher than the chest nor lower than the waist, with the force reaching the heel. The punching force reaches the face of fist and the movements are coordinated. (Fig. 6-9)

图 6-9 蹬腿冲拳
Fig. 6-9 Heel Push Kick and Punch Fist

9. 马步冲拳   Punch Fist in a Horse Stance

要点：转腰顺肩，冲拳快速有力。（图6-10）

Key Points: Turn the waist, extend the shoulder, and punch the fist fast and powerfully. (Fig. 6-10)

图 6-10 马步冲拳
Fig. 6-10 Punch Fist in a Horse Stance

第二段   Section 2

10. 弓步推掌   Push Palm in a Bow Stance

要点：推掌迅速有力，力达小指外沿；推掌与弓步动作协调一致。（图6-11）

Key Points: Push the palm fast and powerfully, with the force reaching the outer edge of the little finger; keep the palm pushing and the bow stance well coordinated. (Fig. 6-11)

图 6-11 弓步推掌
Fig. 6-11 Push Palm in a Bow Stance

11. 拗弓步推掌　　　　　　Push Palm in a Bow Stance (the opposite side)

要点：转腰发力推掌，力达小指外沿；左脚不能拔根或掀脚。（图6-12）

Key Points: Turn the waist and push the palm vigorously, with the force reaching the outer edge of the little finger; the left heel cannot be off the ground or lifted. (Fig. 6-12)

图 6-12　拗弓步推掌
Fig. 6-12 Push Palm in a Bow Stance（the opposite side）

12. 弓步搂手砍掌　　　　Bow Stance with Hand Grabbing and Palm Chopping

要点：转身、搂手、收拳、砍掌动作完成一气呵成，砍掌力达掌外沿。（图6-13）

Key Points: Make the movements non-stop and consistent from turning around, grabbing the hand, withdrawing the fist to chopping the palm. The chopping force reaches the outer edge of the palm. (Fig. 6-13)

图 6-13　弓步搂手砍掌
Fig. 6-13 Bow Stance with Hand Grabbing and Palm Chopping

13. 弓步穿手推掌　　　　　　　Bow Stance with Arm Thrusting and Palm Pushing

要点：推掌力达掌外沿，勾手提腕，指尖向下；手法变换清晰，弓步转换平稳，动作完成协调连贯。（图6-14）

Key Points: The pushing force reaches the outer edge of the palm. Lift the wrist with the hand hooked, fingertips pointing downward; keep the transformation of hand techniques clear, the transition of bow stance smooth, and the movements coherent and coordinated. (Fig. 6-14)

图 6-14　弓步穿手推掌
Fig. 6-14 Bow Stance with Arm Thrusting and Palm Pushing

14. 弓步推掌　　　　　　　　　　　Push Palm in a Bow Stance

要点：手法清晰，力点准确；左弓步时左膝与脚面垂直，大腿呈水平位，右腿扣脚蹬直。（图6-15）

Key Points: Keep the hand techniques clear and the force points accurate; the left knee is perpendicular to the instep in the left bow stance, with the thigh at horizontal level, the right leg straightened, and the toes pointed inward. (Fig. 6-15)

图 6-15　弓步推掌
Fig. 6-15 Push Palm in a Bow Stance

15. 拗弓步推掌　　　　　　　Push Palm in a Bow Stance (the opposite side)

要点：转腰发力推掌，力达小指外沿；左脚不能拔根或掀脚。（图 6-16）

Key Points: Turn the waist and push the palm vigorously, with the force reaching the outer edge of the little finger; the left heel cannot be off the ground or lifted. (Fig. 6-16)

图 6-16　拗弓步推掌
Fig. 6-16　Push Palm in a Bow Stance (the opposite side)

16. 弓步搂手砍掌　　　　Bow Stance with Hand Grabbing and Palm Chopping

要点：转身、搂手、收拳、砍掌动作完成一气呵成，砍掌力达掌外沿。（图6-17）

Key Points: Make the movements non-stop and consistent from turning around, grabbing the hand, withdrawing the fist to chopping the palm. The chopping force reaches the outer edge of the palm. (Fig. 6-17)

图 6-17　弓步搂手砍掌
Fig. 6-17　Bow Stance with Hand Grabbing and Palm Chopping

17. 弓步穿手推掌 Bow Stance with Arm Thrusting and Palm Pushing

要点：推掌力达掌外沿，勾手提腕，指尖向下；手法变换清晰，弓步转换平稳，动作完成协调连贯。（图6-18）

Key Points: The pushing force reaches the outer edge of the palm. Lift the wrist with the hand hooked, fingertips pointing downward; keep the transformation of hand techniques clear, the transition of bow stance smooth, and the movements coherent and coordinated. (Fig. 6-18)

图 6-18 弓步穿手推掌
Fig. 6-18 Bow Stance with Arm Thrusting and Palm Pushing

第三段 Section 3

18. 虚步上架 Uphold Fist in an Empty Stance

要点：上架拳、下栽拳完成迅速；虚步时重心落于左腿，右腿微屈，脚尖点地。（图6-19）

Key Points: Complete the upholding fist and the plunging fist quickly; when making the empty stance, the center of gravity falls onto the left leg, with the right leg slightly bent and the toes touching the ground. (Fig. 6-19)

图 6-19　虚步上架
Fig. 6-19 Uphold Fist in an Empty Stance

19. 马步下压　　　　　　　　　　Strike Arm Downward in a Horse Stance

要点： 两脚换跳灵敏，下砸力达左臂前端。（图6-20）

Key Points: When turning around, switch the footwork swiftly and steadily; make the downward striking force reach the front of the left arm. (Fig. 6-20)

图 6-20　马步下压
Fig. 6-20 Strike Arm Downward in a Horse Stance

20. 拗弓步冲拳   Punch Fist in a Bow Stance (the opposite side)

要点：左弓步时左膝与脚面垂直，大腿呈水平位，右腿蹬直；立拳前冲与弓步动作协调一致。（图6-21）

Key Points: The left knee is perpendicular to the instep in the left bow stance, with the thigh at horizontal level, the right leg straightened, and the toes pointed inward. When punching forward with the upward fist, make the movement well coordinated with the bow stance. (Fig. 6-21)

图 6-21　拗弓步冲拳
Fig. 6-21 Punch Fist in a Bow Stance (the opposite side)

21. 马步冲拳   Punch Fist in a Horse Stance

要点：转腰顺肩，力达拳面；马步与冲拳同时完成。（图6-22）

Key Points: Turn the waist and deliver the shoulder to make the force reach the face of fist, and complete the horse stance and fist punching at the same time. (Fig. 6-22)

图 6-22　马步冲拳
Fig. 6-22 Punch Fist in a Horse Stance

22. 虚步上架 Uphold Fist in an Empty Stance

要点：上架拳、下栽拳完成迅速；虚步时重心落于右腿，左腿微屈，脚尖点地。（图6-23）

Key Points: Complete the upholding fist and the plunging fist quickly; when making the empty stance, the center of gravity falls onto the right leg, with the left leg slightly bent and the toes touching the ground. (Fig. 6-23)

图 6-23　虚步上架
Fig. 6-23 Upholding Fist with Empty Stance

23. 马步下压 Strike Arm Downward in a Horse Stance

要点：两脚换跳轻盈、灵敏，右臂由上向下抡压，力达前臂，动作完成连贯流畅。（图6-24）

Key Points: Switch the footwork lightly and swiftly; press the right arm down from the top with the force reaching the forearm, and keep the movement coherent and smooth. (Fig. 6-24)

图 6-24　马步下压
Fig. 6-24 Strike Arm Downward in a Horse Stance

24. 拗弓步冲拳   Punch Fist in a Bow Stance (the opposite side)

要点：弓步与冲拳动作协调一致，力达拳面。（图6-25）

Key Points: The bow stance and the fist punching are well coordinated, with the force reaching the face of fist. (Fig. 6-25)

图 6-25 拗弓步冲拳

Fig. 6-25 Punch Fist in a Bow Stance (the opposite side)

25. 马步冲拳   Punch Fist in a Horse Stance

要点：冲拳时力达拳面，弓步变马步转换迅速。（图6-26）

Key Points: When punching, the force reaches the face of fist; switch the bow stance to horse stance quickly. (Fig. 6-26)

图 6-26 马步冲拳

Fig. 6-26 Punch Fist in a Horse Stance

第四段　Section 4

26. 弓步双摆掌　　　　　　　Swing Double Palms in a Bow Stance

要点：抡臂、立圆、摆掌，肩关节放松。（图6-27）

Key Points: Swing the arms in a vertical circle and sway the palms, with shoulders relaxed. (Fig. 6-27)

图 6-27　弓步双摆掌
Fig. 6-27 Swing Double Palms in a Bow Stance

27. 弓步撩掌　　　　　　　Scoop Palm in a Bow Stance

要点：左腿蹬地，右腿屈膝前弓成右弓步；左掌前撩，力达掌心；动作连贯，转化快速协调。（图6-28）

Key Points: Stamp the left leg on the ground, bend the right knee forward to form a right bow stance; thrust the left palm forward with the force reaching the center of palm; keep the movements coherent and the transition fast and coordinated. (Fig. 6-28)

图 6-28　弓步撩掌
Fig. 6-28 Scoop Palm in a Bow Stance

28. 推掌弹踢   Push Palm and Spring Kick

要点：弹腿由屈至伸弹出，脚面绷平，力达脚尖；弹腿与推掌动作协调一致。（图6-29）

Key Points: Snap the leg out from bent to full extension with the back of the foot straightened and the force reaching the toes; keep the leg kicking and the palm pushing well coordinated. (Fig. 6-29)

图 6-29　推掌弹踢
Fig. 6-29 Push Palm and Spring Kick

29. 弓步上架推掌   Bow Stance with Arm Upholding and Palm Pushing

要点：右掌上架至头上方，左掌塌腕前推，力达掌外沿；弓步、架掌、推掌动作协调一致，快速有力。（图6-30）

Key Points: Uphold the right palm above the head and push the left palm forward with the wrist down, the force reaching the outer edge of the palm; make the movements of bow stance, palm upholding, and palm pushing coordinated, fast and powerful. (Fig. 6-30)

图 6-30　弓步上架推掌
Fig. 6-30 Bow Stance with Arm Upholding and Palm Pushing

30. 弓步双摆掌   Swing Double Palms in a Bow Stance

要点：转腰摆掌，步型转换迅速；右弓步时右膝与脚面垂直，大腿呈水平位；左脚内扣，膝蹬直；动作协调一致。（图6-31）

Key Points: Turn the waist, sway the palms, and switch the stances quickly; when making the right bow stance, the right knee is perpendicular to the instep, with the thigh at horizontal level; turn the left toes inward and the left knee straightened; keep all the movements well coordinated. (Fig. 6-31)

图 6-31 弓步双摆掌
Fig. 6-31 Swing Double Palms in a Bow Stance

31. 弓步撩掌   Scoop Palm in a Bow Stance

要点：手法清晰，动作连贯，力点准确；上下肢动作协调一致。（图6-32）

Key Points: Keep the hand techniques clear and the movements coherent, the force points accurate, and the movements of upper and lower limbs coordinated. (Fig. 6-32)

图 6-32 弓步撩掌
Fig. 6-32 Scoop Palm in a Bow Stance

32. 推掌弹踢   Push Palm and Spring Kick

要点：推掌、弹踢动作协调一致，推掌力达掌外沿。（图6-33）

Key Points: Keep palm pushing and spring kick coordinated, with the pushing force reaching the outer edge of the palm. (Fig. 6-33)

图 6-33 推掌弹踢
Fig. 6-33 Push Palm and Spring Kick

33. 弓步上架推掌   Bow Stance with Arm Upholding and Palm Pushing

要点：左掌上架至头上方，右掌塌腕前推，力达掌外沿；弓步、架掌、推掌动作协调一致，快速有力。（图6-34）

Key Points: Uphold the left palm above the head and push the right palm forward with the wrist down, the force reaching the outer edge of the palm; make the movements of bow stance, palm upholding, and palm pushing coordinated, fast and powerful. (Fig. 6-34)

图 6-34 弓步上架推掌
Fig. 6-34 Bow Stance with Arm Upholding and Palm Pushing

34. 收势   Closing Posture

要点：头须端正，收下颌，挺胸、立腰、松肩。（图6-35）

Key Points: Keep the head straight, the chin drew inward, the chest out, the waist up, and the shoulders relaxed. (Fig. 6-35)

图 6-35　收势
Fig. 6-35 Closing Posture

练习一段长拳结束后行抱拳礼。

At the end of your practice, perform the palm-fist salute.

二段长拳

技术内容

① 招数：34式。

② 段数：4段。

③ 手型：3种（拳、掌、勾）。

④ 步型：4种（弓步、马步、虚步、歇步）。

⑤ 拳法：3种（冲拳、架拳、砸拳）。

⑥ 掌法：3种（亮掌、推掌、穿掌）。

⑦ 肘法：2种（挎肘、顶肘）。

⑧ 腿法：2种（弹腿、正踢腿）。

⑨ 平衡：1种（提膝平衡）。

⑩ 跳跃：1种（腾空飞脚）。

Technical Contents

① Move: 34 moves.

② Section: 4 sections.

③ Hand Form: 3 hand forms (fist, palm, hook).

④ Stance: 4 stances (bow stance, horse stance, empty stance, resting stance).

⑤ Fist Technique: 3 fists (punching fist, upholding fist, hammer striking fist).

⑥ Palm Technique: 3 palms (showing palm, pushing palm, thrusting palm).

⑦ Elbow Technique: 2 elbows (bending elbow, pushing elbow).

⑧ Leg Technique: 2 legs (spring kick, front kick).

⑨ Balance: 1 balance (knee-raised balance).

⑩ Jumping: 1 kick (flying front kick).

动作名称

预备势

第一段

1. 起势

2. 拗弓步搂手冲拳

3. 冲拳弹踢

4. 马步上架冲拳

5. 虚步挎肘

6. 拗弓步搂手冲拳

7. 冲拳弹踢

8. 马步上架冲拳

9. 虚步挎肘

第二段

10. 歇步亮掌

11. 转身弓步顶肘

12. 提膝双扣拳

13. 弓步双推掌

14. 歇步亮掌

15. 转身弓步顶肘

16. 提膝双扣拳

17. 弓步双推掌

第三段

18. 虚步推掌

19. 歇步抡压

20. 提膝上穿掌

21. 弓步撑掌

22. 虚步推掌

23. 歇步抡压

24. 提膝上穿掌

25. 弓步撑掌

第四段

26. 虚步穿掌

27. 进步踢腿

28. 纵步飞脚

29. 弓步推掌

30. 虚步穿掌

31. 进步踢腿

32. 纵步飞脚

33. 弓步推掌

34. 收势

二段长拳
Chang Quan:
Grade 2

Names of the Movements

Preparatory Posture

Section 1

1. Starting Posture

2. Bow Stance with Hand Grabbing and Fist Punching (the opposite side)

3. Punch Fist and Spring Kick

4. Horse Stance with Fist Upholding and Punching

5. Bend Elbow in an Empty Stance

6. Bow Stance with Hand Grabbing and Fist Punching (the opposite side)

7. Punch Fist and Spring Kick

8. Horse Stance with Fist Upholding and Punching

9. Bend Elbow in an Empty Stance

Section 2

10. Show Palm in a Resting Stance

11. Turn Body and Push Elbow in a Bow Stance

12. Both Fists Horizontally Aligned with Knee Raised

13. Push Double Palms in a Bow Stance

14. Show Palm in a Resting Stance

15. Turn Body and Push Elbow in a Bow Stance

16. Both Fists Horizontally Aligned with Knee Raised

17. Push Double Palms in a Bow Stance

Section 3

18. Push Palm in an Empty Stance

19. Swing Arm and Press Fist Downward in a Resting Stance

20. Uplift Knee and Thrust Palm Upward

21. Stretch Palms in a Bow Stance

22. Push Palm in an Empty Stance

23. Swing Arm and Press Fist Downward in a Resting Stance

24. Uplift Knee and Thrust Palm Upward

25. Stretch Palms in a Bow Stance

Section 4

26. Thrust Palm in an Empty Stance

27. Kick Leg in an Advancing Step

28. Fly Foot in a Hopping Step

29. Push Palm in a Bow Stance

30. Thrust Palm in an Empty Stance

31. Kick Leg in an Advancing Step

32. Fly Foot in a Hopping Step

33. Push Palm in a Bow Stance

34. Closing Posture

练习二段长拳开始前行抱拳礼。

Before your practice, perform the palm-fist salute.

预备势   Preparatory Posture

要点：挺胸、收腹、立腰，头正颈直。（图6-36）

Key Points: Keep the chest out, the abdomen in, the waist up, the head upright and the neck straight. (Fig. 6-36)

第一段 Section 1

1. 起势   Starting Posture

要点：挺胸立腰，两肘后夹，两拳紧贴腰侧，拳心向上。（图6-37）

Key Points: Keep the chest high and the waist erected, two elbows tucked backward, two fists close to the waist and the heart of fist pointing upward. (Fig. 6-37)

图 6-36　预备势
Fig. 6-36 Preparatory Posture

图 6-37　起势
Fig. 6-37 Starting Posture

2.拗弓步搂手冲拳　Bow Stance with Hand Grabbing and Fist Punching (the opposite side)

要点：左弓步时左膝与脚面垂直，大腿呈水平位；右脚内扣，右膝伸直；冲拳与弓步动作协调一致，力达拳面。（图6-38）

Key Points: The left knee is perpendicular to the instep in the left bow stance, with the thigh at horizontal level; turn the right toes inward and straighten the right knee; keep the fist punching and the bow stance well coordinated, with the force reaching the face of fist. (Fig. 6-38)

图 6-38　拗弓步搂手冲拳

Fig. 6-38　Bow Stance with Hand Grabbing and Fist Punching (the opposite side)

3.冲拳弹踢　Punch Fist and Spring Kick

要点：弹腿时由屈至伸弹出，脚面绷平，力达脚尖；弹腿与冲拳动作协调一致。（图6-39）

Key Points: When making the spring kick from bent to full extension, straighten the back of foot with the force reaching the toes; keep the spring kick and fist punching well coordinated. (Fig. 6-39)

图 6-39　冲拳弹踢

Fig. 6-39　Punch Fist and Spring Kick

4. 马步上架冲拳   Horse Stance with Fist Upholding and Punching

要点： 马步与冲拳、架拳动作协调一致，快速有力。（图6-40）

Key Points: Keep the horse stance, fist upholding and fist punching well coordinated, fast and powerful. (Fig. 6-40)

图 6-40　马步上架冲拳
Fig. 6-40　Horse Stance with Fist Upholding and Punching

5. 虚步挎肘   Bend Elbow in an Empty Stance

要点： 步型转换迅速，成右虚步时脚尖点地；挎肘时上臂与前臂屈成直角或稍大于直角。（图6-41）

Key Points: Switch the stances quickly, with the right toes touching the ground in the right bow stance; when bending the elbow, bend the upper arm and the forearm into a right angle or slightly larger than the right angle. (Fig. 6-41)

图 6-41　虚步挎肘
Fig. 6-41　Bend Elbow in an Empty Stance

6. 拗弓步搂手冲拳　　Bow Stance with Hand Grabbing and Fist Punching (the opposite side)

要点：动作协调一致，快速敏捷。（图6-42）

Key Points: Keep the movements well coordinated, fast and agile. (Fig. 6-42)

图 6-42　拗弓步搂手冲拳
Fig. 6-42 Bow Stance with Hand Grabbing and Fist Punching (the opposite side)

7. 冲拳弹踢　　Punch Fist and Spring Kick

要点：上下肢动作配合协调一致，冲拳力达拳面。（图6-43）

Key Points: Keep the movements of the upper and lower limbs well coordinated, with the punching force reaching the face of fist. (Fig. 6-43)

图 6-43　冲拳弹踢
Fig. 6-43 Punch Fist and Spring Kick

8. 马步上架冲拳　　　　　　　　Horse Stance with Fist Upholding and Punching

要点：发力顺达，力点准确；上下肢动作协调一致。（图6-44）

Key Points: Keep the force smooth, the force points accurate, and the movements of upper and lower limbs well coordinated. (Fig. 6-44)

图 6-44　马步上架冲拳
Fig. 6-44 Horse Stance with Fist Upholding and Punching

9. 虚步挎肘　　　　　　　　　　　　　Bend Elbow in an Empty Stance

要点：成左虚步时，重心落于右腿，左腿微屈，脚尖点地。（图6-45）

Key Points: The center of gravity falls onto the right leg in left empty stance; slightly bend the left leg with the toes touching the ground. (Fig. 6-45)

图 6-45　虚步挎肘
Fig. 6-45 Bend Elbow in an Empty Stance

第二段 Section 2

10. 歇步亮掌 Show Palm in a Resting Stance

要点： 右手抖腕亮掌；成歇步时两腿交叉屈膝全蹲，左脚全脚掌着地，脚尖外展，右脚跟离地，臀部坐于小腿上。（图6-46）

Key Points: Shake the right wrist and show the palm; when making a cross-legged crouching stance, cross both legs with knees bent to form a full squat and the sole of the left foot is on the ground; with the toes outstretched, the right heel is off the ground and the buttocks sit on the calf. (Fig. 6-46)

图 6-46 歇步亮掌
Fig. 6-46 Show Palm in a Resting Stance

11. 转身弓步顶肘 Turn Body and Push Elbow in a Bow Stance

要点： 转身上步，步法灵活；上下肢动作配合协调一致。（图6-47）

Key Points: Turn around and step forward with flexible footwork; keep the movements of the upper and lower limbs well coordinated. (Fig. 6-47)

图 6-47　转身弓步顶肘
Fig. 6-47 Turn Body and Push Elbow in a Bow Stance

12. 提膝双扣拳　　　　　Both Fists Horizontally Aligned with Knee Raised

要点：扣拳力达拳背，从上向下猛然伸肘、甩臂，扣拳平举之后，肘微屈。（图6-48）

Key Points: When pressing the fists downward, the force reaches the back of fist. After you suddenly stretch the elbows, throw the arms from top to bottom, and press the fists downward with two fists horizontally aligned, slightly bend the elbows. (Fig. 6-48)

图 6-48　提膝双扣拳
Fig. 6-48 Both Fists Horizontally Aligned with Knee Raised

13. 弓步双推掌   Push Double Palms in a Bow Stance

要点：震脚和按掌、弓步和推掌动作协调一致。（图6-49）

Key Points: Keep foot stamping, palm pressing, bow stance and palm pushing well coordinated. (Fig. 6-49)

图 6-49　弓步双推掌
Fig. 6-49 Push Double Palms in a Bow Stance

14. 歇步亮掌   Show Palm in a Resting Stance

要点：抖腕亮掌，手法清晰；上下肢动作协调一致。（图6-50）

Key Points: Keep the hand techniques clear when shaking the wrist and showing the palm, and keep the movements of the upper and lower limbs well coordinated. (Fig. 6-50)

图 6-50　歇步亮掌
Fig. 6-50 Show Palm in a Resting Stance

15. 转身弓步顶肘　　　　　　Turn Body and Push Elbow in a Bow Stance

要点：步法灵活，动作连贯；弓步与顶肘动作协调一致。（图6-51）

Key Points: Keep the footwork flexible and movements consistent and make the bow stance and elbow pushing well coordinated. (Fig. 6-51)

图 6-51　转身弓步顶肘
Fig. 6-51 Turn Body and Push Elbow in a Bow Stance

16. 提膝双扣拳　　　　　　　Both Fists Horizontally Aligned with Knee Raised

要点：提膝快速敏捷，支撑稳定。（图6-52）

Key Points: Uplift the knee quickly and agilely; keep the support stable. (Fig. 6-52)

图 6-52　提膝双扣拳
Fig. 6-52 Both Fists Horizontally Aligned with Knee Raised

17. 弓步双推掌　　　　　　　Push Double Palms in a Bow Stance

要点：手法清晰，力点准确；左弓步时左膝与脚背垂直，大腿呈水平位，右腿扣脚蹬直。（图6-53）

Key Points: Keep the hand techniques clear and the force points accurate; the left knee is perpendicular to the instep in the left bow stance, with the thigh at horizontal level; the right leg is straightened with the toes pointed inward. (Fig. 6-53)

图 6-53　弓步双推掌
Fig. 6-53 Push Double Palms in a Bow Stance

第三段 Section 3

18. 虚步推掌   Push Palm in an Empty Stance

要点：推掌力达掌外沿，勾手时指尖向下；上下肢动作协调一致。
（图6-54）

Key Points: The pushing force reaches the outer edge of the palm; when hooking the hand, the fingertips are downward; keep the movements of the upper and lower limbs well coordinated. (Fig. 6-54)

图 6-54　虚步推掌
Fig. 6-54 Push Palm in an Empty Stance

19. 歇步抡压　　　　Swing Arm and Press Fist Downward in a Resting Stance

要点：抡臂立圆，动作连贯；歇步时两腿交叉全蹲；动作完成迅速。
（图6-55）

Key Points: Swing the arms in a vertical circle with the movements coherent; when making the resting stance, cross both legs to form a full squat, completing the movement quickly. (Fig. 6-55)

图 6-55　歇步抡压
Fig. 6-55 Swing Arm and Press Fist Downward in a Resting Stance

20. 提膝上穿掌　　　　　　　Uplift Knee and Thrust Palm Upward

要点：上穿与下穿动作同时进行，连贯协调。（图6-56）

Key Points: The upward and downward thrusting are carried out at the same time, coherent and coordinated. (Fig. 6-56)

图 6-56　提膝上穿掌
Fig. 6-56 Uplift Knee and Thrust Palm Upward

21. 弓步撑掌　　　　　　　　　　　　　　Stretch Palms in a Bow Stance

要点：推掌力达掌外沿，两肩松沉，动作连贯。（图6-57）

Key Points: The pushing force reaches the outer edge of the palm with both shoulders relaxed and the movements coherent. (Fig. 6-57)

图 6-57　弓步撑掌
Fig. 6-57 Stretch Palms in a Bow Stance

22. 虚步推掌   Push Palm in an Empty Stance

要点：成虚步时，重心落于右腿，左腿微屈，脚尖点地；虚步与推掌动作协调一致。（图6–58）

Key Points: The center of gravity falls onto the right leg in an empty stance; slightly bend the left leg with the toes on the ground; complete the empty stance and palm pushing at the same time. (Fig. 6-58)

图6–58　虚步推掌
Fig. 6-58 Push Palm in an Empty Stance

23. 歇步抡压   Swing Arm and Press Fist Downward in a Resting Stance

要点：抡压力达拳背，歇步时臀部坐于右小腿上；上下肢动作配合协调一致，动作完成迅速。（图6–59）

Key Points: The throwing and pressing force reaches the back of fist, and the buttocks sit on the right calf when making the resting stance. The movements of the upper and lower limbs are coordinated and completed quickly. (Fig. 6-59)

图 6-59　歇步抢压
Fig. 6-59 Swing Arm and Press Fist Downward in a Resting Stance

24. 提膝上穿掌　　　　　　　　　　　　Uplift Knee and Thrust Palm Upward

　　要点：左掌直立上穿，提膝迅速，气息下沉，支撑稳定，上体保持直立。（图6-60）

Key Points: Raise the left palm upright with the knee lifted quickly, and keep the breath down, the support stable and the upper body upright. (Fig. 6-60)

图 6-60　提膝上穿掌
Fig. 6-60 Uplift Knee and Thrust Palm Upward

25. 弓步撑掌   Stretch Palms in a Bow Stance

要点：两掌指尖向上，力达掌外沿；右弓步时右膝与脚背垂直，大腿呈水平位；左腿蹬直，脚尖内扣。（图6-61）

Key Points: The fingertips of both palms are upward, and the force reaches the outer edge of the palm; the right knee is perpendicular to the instep in the right bow stance, with the thigh at horizontal level; straighten the left leg with the toes pointed inward. (Fig. 6-61)

图 6-61　弓步撑掌
Fig. 6-61　Stretch Palms in a Bow Stance

第四段   Section 4

26. 虚步穿掌   Thrust Palm in an Empty Stance

要点：收拳、穿掌、虚步动作协调一致，穿掌力达指尖。（图6-62）

Key Points: Keep fist retracting, palm thrusting, and the empty stance well coordinated, with the piercing force reaching the fingertips. (Fig. 6-62)

图 6-62　虚步穿掌
Fig. 6-62 Thrust Palm in an Empty Stance

27. 进步踢腿　　　　　　　　　　　　Kick Leg in an Advancing Step

要点：右手上架至头顶上方，踢腿时两膝尽量伸直，踢摆迅速。（图 6-63）

Key Points: Uphold the right hand to the top of the head; straighten both knees when kicking; keep the kick swift. (Fig. 6-63)

图 6-63　进步踢腿
Fig. 6-63 Kick Leg in an Advancing Step

28.纵步飞脚   Fly Foot in a Hopping Step

要点：击响腿脚尖过肩，右腿提膝收于腹前；空中立身击掌，拍脚迅速准确。（图6-64）

Key Points: Toes of the slapping leg go above the shoulder; lift the right knee up, close to the front of the abdomen; keep the body upright and clap the palms in the air; slap the foot quickly and accurately. (Fig. 6-64)

图 6-64　纵步飞脚
Fig. 6-64 Fly Foot in a Hopping Step

29.弓步推掌   Push Palm in a Bow Stance

要点：左脚前落成左弓步，推掌、转腰、顺肩，力达掌外沿，弓步与推掌动作协调一致。（图6-65）

Key Points: Land the left foot forward into a left bow stance; push the palm, turn the waist, and extend the shoulder, making the force reach the outer edge of the palm; keep the bow stance and palm pushing well coordinated. (Fig. 6-65)

图 6-65　弓步推掌
Fig. 6-65　Push Palm in a Bow Stance

30. 虚步穿掌　　　　　　　　　　　　Thrust Palm in an Empty Stance

要点： 收拳、穿掌、虚步动作协调一致，穿掌力达指尖。（图6-66）

Key Points: Keep fist retracting, palm thrusting, and the empty stance well coordinated, with the thrusting force reaching the fingertips. (Fig. 6-66)

图 6-66　虚步穿掌
Fig. 6-66　Thrust Palm in an Empty Stance

31. 进步踢腿   Kick Leg in an Advancing Step

要点：左掌上架至头顶上方；右腿上踢时，脚尖勾起；左腿接近伸直，上体保持正直。（图6-67）

Key Points: Uphold the left hand to the top of the head; when kicking the right leg, make the toes hooked up; straighten the left leg and keep the upper body straight. (Fig. 6-67)

图 6-67　进步踢腿
Fig. 6-67 Kick Leg in an Advancing Step

32. 纵步飞脚   Fly Foot in a Hopping Step

要点：右脚蹬地起跳，空中立身击掌，拍脚迅速准确，上下肢动作协调一致。（图6-68）

Key Points: Jump into the air with a drive of the right foot; keep the body upright and clap the palms in the air; slap the foot quickly and accurately; keep the movements of upper and lower limbs coordinated. (Fig. 6-68)

图 6-68　纵步飞脚
Fig. 6-68 Fly Foot in a Hopping Step

33. 弓步推掌　　　　　　　　　　　　　　Push Palm in a Bow Stance

要点：右脚前落成右弓步，推掌、转腰、顺肩，力达掌外沿，弓步与推掌动作协调一致。（图6-69）

Key Points: Land the right foot forward into a right bow stance; push the palm, turn the waist, and extend the shoulder, making the force reach the outer edge of the palm; and keep the bow stance and palm pushing well coordinated. (Fig. 6-69)

图 6-69　弓步推掌
Fig. 6-69 Push Palm in a Bow Stance

34. 收势   Closing Posture

要点： 头正颈直，收下颌，挺胸，立腰，沉肩。（图6-70）

Key Points: Keep the head straight, the chin drew inward, the chest out, the waist up, and the shoulders dropped. (Fig. 6-70)

图 6-70　收势
Fig. 6-70 Closing Posture

练习二段长拳结束后行抱拳礼。

At the end of your practice, perform the palm-fist salute.

三段长拳 Chang Quan: Grade 3

技术内容

① 招数：34式。

② 段数：4段。

③ 手型：3种（拳、掌、勾）。

④ 步型：6种（弓步、虚步、马步、仆步、歇步、叉步）。

⑤ 拳法：5种（冲拳、栽拳、砸拳、劈拳、挑拳）。

⑥ 掌法：7种（穿掌、亮掌、按掌、推掌、摆掌、挑掌、劈掌）。

⑦ 肘法：3种（格肘、盘肘、顶肘）。

⑧ 腿法：4种（弹腿、正踢腿、侧踹腿、单拍脚）。

⑨ 步法：2种（跃步、插步）。

⑩ 跳跃：1种（飞脚）。

Technical Contents

① Move: 34 moves.

② Section: 4 sections.

③ Hand Form: 3 hand forms (fist, palm, hook).

④ Stance: 6 stances (bow stance, empty stance, horse stance, crouching stance, resting stance, Y-shaped stance).

⑤ Fist Technique: 5 fists (punching fist, plunging fist, hammer striking fist, chopping fist, uplifting fist).

⑥ Palm Technique: 7 palms (thrusting palm, showing palm, pressing palm, pushing palm, swing palm, uplifting palm, hacking palm).

⑦ Elbow Technique: 3 elbows (blocking elbow, hook elbow, pushing elbow).

⑧ Leg Technique: 4 legs (spring kick, front kick, side kick, single foot slap).

⑨ Footwork: 2 footwork (leaping step, back cross stance).

⑩ Jumping: 1kick (flying front kick).

动作名称

预备势

第一段

1. 起势

2. 弓步冲拳

3. 弹腿冲拳

4. 马步冲拳

5. 弓步冲拳

6. 弹腿冲拳

7. 大跃步前穿

8. 弓步击掌

9. 马步架掌

第二段

10. 虚步栽拳

11. 提膝穿掌

12. 仆步穿掌

13. 虚步挑掌

14. 马步击掌

15. 叉步双摆掌

16. 弓步击掌

17. 转身踢腿马步盘肘

第三段

18. 歇步抡砸拳

19. 仆步亮掌

20. 弓步劈拳

21. 换跳步弓步冲拳

22. 马步冲拳

23. 弓步下冲掌

24. 叉步亮掌侧踹腿

25. 虚步挑拳

第四段

26. 弓步顶肘

27. 转身左拍脚

28. 右拍脚

29. 腾空飞脚

30. 歇步下冲拳

31. 仆步抡劈拳

32. 提膝挑掌

33. 提膝劈掌弓步冲拳

34. 收势

三段长拳
Chang Quan:
Grade 3

Names of Movements

Preparatory Posture

Section 1

1. Starting Posture

2. Punch Fist in a Bow Stance

3. Spring Kick and Punch Fist

4. Punch Fist in a Horse Stance

5. Punch Fist in a Bow Stance

6. Spring Kick and Punch Fist

7. Forward Giant Leap

8. Strike Palm in a Bow Stance

9. Uphold Palm in a Horse Stance

Section 2

10. Plunge Fist in an Empty Stance

11. Uplift Knee and Thrust Palm

12. Thrust Palm in a Crouching Stance

13. Uplift Palm in an Empty Stance

14. Strike Palm in a Horse Stance

15. Swing Double Palms in a Y-shaped Stance

16. Strike Palm in a Bow Stance

17. Turn Body, Kick Leg, Hook Elbow in a Horse Stance

Section 3

18. Swing Arms to Strike Fists in a Resting Stance

19. Show Palm in a Crouching Stance

20. Chop Fist in a Bow Stance

21. Shift Steps and Punch Fist in a Bow Stance

22. Punch Fist in a Horse Stance

23. Thrust Palm Downward in a Bow Stance

24. Show Palm in a Y-shaped Stance with Side Kick

25. Uplift Fist in an Empty Stance

Section 4

26. Push Elbow in a Bow Stance

27. Turn Body and Slap Left Foot

28. Slap Right Foot

29. Flying Front Kick

30. Punch Fist Downward in a Resting Stance

31. Swing and Chop Fist in a Crouching Stance

32. Uplift Palm with Knee Raised

33. Uplift Knee with Palm Hacking and Punch Fist in a Bow Stance

34. Closing Posture

练习三段长拳开始前行抱拳礼。

Before your practice, perform the palm-fist salute.

预备势   Preparatory Posture

要点：头正颈直，下颌微收，挺胸收腹。（图6-71）

Key Points: Keep the head upright and the neck straight, the chin slightly drew inward, the chest out and the abdomen in. (Fig. 6-71)

图 6-71　预备势
Fig. 6-71 Preparatory Posture

第一段　Section 1

1.起势   Starting Posture

（1）虚步亮掌

要点：左掌沿右臂上穿后摆至体后勾手，指尖向上；虚步时重心在右腿，屈蹲至水平位置；虚步、摆头、亮掌动作连贯，协调一致。（图6-72）

(1) Show Palm in an Empty Stance

Key Points: Thrust the left palm upward along the right arm, then swing it to the back of the body, and make the hand hooked with fingertips pointing upward; when making the empty stance, move the center of gravity to the right foot, and squat to horizontal level; keep the empty stance, head swinging and palm showing coherent and coordinated. (Fig. 6-72)

图 6-72　虚步亮掌
Fig. 6-72 Show Palm in an Empty Stance

（2）并步对拳

要点：连续上步迅速，对拳、摆头同时完成，动作连贯，上下肢动作配合协调一致。（图6-73）

(2) Stand with Feet Together and Fist to Fist

Key Points: Continue to step up quickly, complete punching with fists opposite and the head swinging at the same time, and keep the movements coherent, upper and lower limbs well coordinated. (Fig. 6-73)

图 6-73　并步对拳
Fig. 6-73 Stand with Feet Together and Fist to Fist

2. 弓步冲拳   Punch Fist in a Bow Stance

要点：左弓步时左膝与脚面垂直，大腿呈水平位，右脚尖内扣，右膝伸直；冲拳与弓步协调一致，力达拳面。（图6-74）

Key Points: The left knee is perpendicular to the instep in the left bow stance, with the thigh at horizontal level; turn the right toes inward and straighten the right knee; keep the fist punching and the bow stance well coordinated, with the force reaching the face of fist. (Fig. 6-74)

图 6-74　弓步冲拳
Fig. 6-74　Punch Fist in a Bow Stance

3. 弹腿冲拳   Spring Kick and Punch Fist

要点：右弹腿由屈至伸弹出，脚面绷平，力达脚尖；弹腿与冲拳动作协调一致。（图6-75）

Key Points: When making the right Spring kick from bent to full extension, straighten the back of foot with the force reaching the toes; keep the spring kick and fist punching well coordinated. (Fig. 6-75)

图 6-75　弹腿冲拳
Fig. 6-75　Spring Kick and Punch Fist

4. 马步冲拳   Punch Fist in a Horse Stance

要点： 上体左转，右腿下落成马步，马步与冲拳同时完成，冲拳力达拳面。（图6-76）

Key Points: The upper body turns left, and the right leg falls into a horse stance; complete the horse stance and fist punching at the same time, with the punching force reaching the face of fist. (Fig. 6-76)

图 6-76　马步冲拳
Fig. 6-76　Punch Fist in a Horse Stance

5. 弓步冲拳   Punch Fist in a Bow Stance

要点： 格挡冲拳快速连贯；右弓步时右膝与脚面垂直，左腿绷直。（图6-77）

Key Points: Make the blocking and punching quick and consistent; when making the right bow stance, the right knee is perpendicular to the instep and the left leg is straight. (Fig. 6-77)

图 6-77　弓步冲拳
Fig. 6-77　Punch Fist in a Bow Stance

6. 弹腿冲拳　　　　　　　　　　　　　Spring Kick and Punch Fist

要点：左弹腿由屈至伸弹出，脚面绷平，力达脚尖；弹腿与冲拳动作协调一致。（图6-78）

Key Points: When making the left Spring kick from bent to full extension, straighten the back of foot with the force reaching the toes; keep the spring kick and fist punching well coordinated. (Fig. 6-78)

图 6-78　弹腿冲拳
Fig. 6-78　Spring Kick and Punch Fist

7. 大跃步前穿　　　　　　　　　　　　Forward Giant Leap

要点：左腿屈膝回收提膝，重心平稳；跃步步法敏捷，空中展身摆掌；上下肢动作配合协调一致。（图6-79）

Key Points: Bend the left knee, draw it back and raise it up with the center of gravity stable; with the agile leaping step, stretch the body and swing the palm in the air; keep the movements of the upper and lower limbs well coordinated. (Fig. 6-79)

图 6-79　大跃步前穿
Fig. 6-79 Forward Giant Leap

8. 弓步击掌　　　　　　　　　　　　　　Strike Palm in a Bow Stance

要点：重心前移成左弓步，右膝伸直，右脚内扣；推掌力达掌外沿。
（图6-80）

Key Points: Move the center of gravity forward into a left bow stance and straighten the right knee with right toes pointed inward; the pushing force reaches the outer edge of the palm. (Fig. 6-80)

图 6-80　弓步击掌
Fig. 6-80 Strike Palm in a Bow Stance

9. 马步架掌   Uphold Palm in a Horse Stance

要点： 左掌摆至头顶上方架掌；成马步时两膝外撑，大腿呈水平位；上下肢动作协调一致。（图6-81）

Key Points: Uphold the left palm to the top of the head; when making the horse stance, the two knees are outwardly supported, with the thigh at horizontal level, and the movements of the upper and lower limbs coordinated. (Fig. 6-81)

图 6-81　马步架掌
Fig. 6-81 Uphold Palm in a Horse Stance

第二段　Section 2

10. 虚步栽拳   Plunge Fist in an Empty Stance

要点： 左栽拳拳面向下；成虚步时重心在右腿，左脚虚点；上架拳与下栽拳动作协调一致。（图6-82）

Key Points: The face of left plunging fist points downward; when making the empty stance, the center of gravity falls onto the right leg, with the left toes lightly touching the ground; keep the fist upholding and downward plunging well coordinated. (Fig. 6-82)

图 6-82　虚步栽拳
Fig. 6-82 Plunge Fist in an Empty Stance

11. 提膝穿掌　　　　　　　　　　　　　Uplift Knee and Thrust Palm

要点：右掌沿左掌之上穿出；左腿收膝上提，右腿伸直；提膝与穿掌动作协调一致。（图6-83）

Key Points: Thrust the right palm out along the back of left palm; retract the left leg, raise the left knee up and straighten the right leg; keep the knee uplifting and palm thrusting well coordinated. (Fig. 6-83)

图 6-83　提膝穿掌
Fig. 6-83 Uplift Knee and Thrust Palm

12. 仆步穿掌   Thrust Palm in a Crouching Stance

要点：右腿屈膝全蹲，左腿平铺，左掌沿左腿内侧向前穿出；重心前移顺畅。（图6-84）

Key Points: Bend the right knee to form a full squat, with the left leg horizontally straightened; thrust the left palm forward along the inner side of the left leg with the center of gravity moving forward smoothly. (Fig. 6-84)

图 6-84　仆步穿掌
Fig. 6-84 Thrust Palm in a Crouching Stance

13. 虚步挑掌   Uplift Palm in an Empty Stance

要点：右掌塌腕挑起；成虚步时重心在左腿，右脚尖虚点；虚步与挑掌动作协调一致。（图6-85）

Key Points: Press the center of right palm downward to form a Uplifting Palm; when making the empty stance, the center of gravity falls on the left leg with the right toes lightly touching the ground; keep the empty stance and palm uplifting well coordinated. (Fig. 6-85)

图 6-85　虚步挑掌
Fig. 6-85 Uplift Palm in an Empty Stance

14. 马步击掌 Strike Palm in a Horse Stance

要点：击掌力达掌外沿。（图6-86）

Key Points: The striking force reaches the outer edge of the palm. (Fig. 6-86)

图 6-86　马步击掌
Fig. 6-86 Strike Palm in a Horse Stance

15. 叉步双摆掌 Swing Double Palms in a Y-shaped Stance

要点：立圆、抡臂、双摆掌；插步迅速，摆掌与后插步动作协调一致。（图6-87）

Key Points: Swing the arms in a vertical circle with palms swaying; make the back cross stance fast; keep the palm swaying and back cross stance well coordinated. (Fig. 6-87)

图 6-87　叉步双摆掌
Fig. 6-87 Swing Double Palms in a Y-shaped Stance

16. 弓步击掌 Strike Palm in a Bow Stance

要点：左脚后撤步成右弓步，左脚尖内扣，膝蹬直；推掌力达掌外沿。（图6-88）

Key Points: Step backward with the left foot into a right bow stance, with the left foot pointed inward and the knee straightened; the pushing force reaches the outer edge of the palm. (Fig. 6-88)

图 6-88　弓步击掌
Fig. 6-88　Strike Palm in a Bow Stance

17. 转身踢腿马步盘肘 Turn Body, Kick Leg, Hook Elbow in a Horse Stance

要点：踢腿时，左掌上架至头顶上方，踢摆迅速，动作连贯。（图6-89）

Key Points: When kicking the leg, uphold the left palm to the top of the head and kick swiftly with coherent movements. (Fig. 6-89)

图 6-89　转身踢腿马步盘肘
Fig. 6-89 Turn Body, Kick Leg, Hook Elbow in a Horse Stance

第三段　Section 3

18. 歇步抡砸拳　　　　　　　　　Swing Arms to Strike Fists in a Resting Stance

要点：抡臂立圆，砸拳力达左拳背；成歇步时两腿交叉全蹲；动作完成连贯，一气呵成。（图6-90）

Key Points: Swing the arm in a vertical circle then strike it down, with the force reaching the back of left fist; cross legs and squat, making the cross-legged crouching stance with coherent and consistent movements. (Fig. 6-90)

图 6-90　歇步抡砸拳
Fig. 6-90 Swing Arms to Strike Fists in a Resting Stance

19. 仆步亮掌   Show Palm in a Crouching Stance

要点：右掌在头顶上方抖腕亮掌；成仆步时挺胸、立腰，平铺腿伸直，脚尖内扣，屈蹲腿全蹲。（图6-91）

Key Points: Shake the wrist with the right palm above the head to show the palm; when making the crouching stance, keep the chest out, the waist up, the horizontally stretched leg straightened, toes turned inward and the squatting leg fully squatted. (Fig. 6-91)

图 6-91　仆步亮拳
Fig. 6-91 Show Palm in a Crouching Stance

20. 弓步劈拳   Chop Fist in a Bow Stance

要点：左、右脚上步稍带弧形，劈拳力达拳背。（图6-92）

Key Points: Step forward in a slightly curved path with both feet and the chopping force reaches the back of fist. (Fig. 6-92)

图 6-92　弓步劈拳
Fig. 6-92 Chop Fist in a Bow Stance

21. 换跳步弓步冲拳　　　　　Shift Steps and Punch Fist in a Bow Stance

要点：换跳步动作连贯、协调，震脚时腿微屈，全脚掌着地；冲拳力达拳面。（图6-93）

Key Points: When shifting steps, make the movements coherent and coordinated; when stamping the foot, slightly bend the leg, with the sole of the foot on the ground; make the punching force reach the face of fist. (Fig. 6-93)

图 6-93　换跳步弓步冲拳
Fig. 6-93 Shift Steps and Punch Fist in a Bow Stance

22. 马步冲拳   Punch Fist in a Horse Stance

要点：步型转换迅速，冲拳时转腰顺肩，力达拳面。（图6-94）

Key Points: Switch the stances quickly; when punching the fist, turn the waist and extend the shoulder, making the force reach the face of fist. (Fig. 6-94)

图 6-94　马步冲拳

Fig. 6-94 Punch Fist in a Horse Stance

23. 弓步下冲掌   Thrust Palm Downward in a Bow Stance

要点：以腰带臂，左掌摆至头上方架掌，右拳向右前下方冲出，力达拳面；上下肢动作配合一致，马步转弓步迅速完成。（图6-95）

Key Points: Drive the arm with the waist, swing the left palm to the top of the head and parry with the palm; thrust out the right fist to the right lower front, with the force reaching the face of fist; keep the movements of the upper and lower limbs coordinated and switch the horse stance to bow stance quickly. (Fig. 6-95)

图 6-95　弓步下冲掌

Fig. 6-95 Thrust Palm Downward in a Bow Stance

24. 叉步亮掌侧踹腿　　　　Show Palm in a Y-shaped Stance with Side Kick

要点：右脚向左脚左后方插出，右腿支撑直立，左腿展胯向左侧挺膝踹出，力达脚跟。（图6-96）

Key Points: Insert the right foot to the left rear of the left foot, stand upright with the right leg, extend the hip with the left leg and kick the leg out to the left with the knee straightened and the force reaching the heel. (Fig. 6-96)

图 6-96　叉步亮掌侧踹腿
Fig. 6-96 Show Palm in a Y-shaped Stance with Side Kick

25. 虚步挑拳   Uplift Fist in an Empty Stance

要点：左脚前落，右脚尖向前虚点成右虚步；左腿屈蹲，大腿接近水平位；虚步与挑拳动作配合协调一致。（图6-97）

Key Points: The left foot falls forward, and the right toes move forward to form a right empty stance; bend the left leg to squat with the thigh at horizontal level; keep the empty stance and the snap fist well coordinated. (Fig. 6-97)

图 6-97　虚步挑拳
Fig. 6-97 Uplift Fist in an Empty Stance

第四段　Section 4

26. 弓步顶肘　　　　　　　　　　　　　　　Push Elbow in a Bow Stance

要点：交换步时灵敏迅速，两臂立圆抡摆，顶肘时力达肘尖。（图6-98）

Key Points: When changing the steps, make the movements agile and quick; swing the arms in a vertical circle; when pushing the elbow, the force reaches the tip of the elbow. (Fig. 6-98)

图 6-98　弓步顶肘
Fig. 6-98 Push Elbow in a Bow Stance

27. 转身左拍脚   Turn Body and Slap Left Foot

要点：身体挺胸直立，上步击拍迅速、准确；上下肢动作配合协调一致。（图6-99）

Key Points: Stand upright with the chest out, step forward and slap quickly and accurately, and keep the movements of the upper and lower limbs well coordinated. (Fig. 6-99)

图 6-99　转身左拍脚
Fig. 6-99 Turn Body and Slap Left Foot

28. 右拍脚   Slap Right Foot

要点：身体挺胸直立，上步击拍迅速、准确；上下肢动作配合协调一致。（图6-100）

Key Points: Stand upright with the chest out, step forward and slap quickly and accurately, and keep the movements of the upper and lower limbs well coordinated. (Fig. 6-100)

图 6-100　右拍脚
Fig. 6-100 Slap Right Foot

29. 腾空飞脚　　　　　　　　　　　　　　　　　　Flying Front Kick

要点：腾空后右腿前上方弹击响腿，脚尖过肩，左腿提膝收于腹前；空中立身击掌，拍脚迅速准确。（图6-101）

Key Points: After jumping into the air, spring kick and slap the right leg in the upper front with the toes over the shoulder and the left leg raised close to the front of abdomen; keep the body upright and clap the palms in the air; slap the foot quickly and accurately. (Fig. 6-101)

图 6-101　腾空飞脚
Fig. 6-101 Flying Front Kick

30. 歇步下冲拳   Punch Fist Downward in a Resting Stance

要点：上体右转，两腿交叉全蹲成歇步；冲拳时转腰顺肩，力达拳面，动作迅速完成。（图6-102）

Key Points: Turn the upper body to the right, cross the legs and squat to form a resting stance; when punching, turn the waist and extend the shoulder, making the force reach the face of fist and the movement complete quickly. (Fig. 6-102)

图 6-102　歇步下冲拳
Fig. 6-102 Punch Fist Downward in a Resting Stance

31. 仆步抡劈拳   Swing and Chop Fist in a Crouching Stance

要点：转身立圆抡劈，力达拳轮；成仆步时挺胸、立腰，右腿平铺伸直，脚尖内扣，左腿屈膝全蹲。（图6-103）

Key Points: Turn around and swing the arms in a vertical circle with fists chopping downward, the force reaching the fist curve; keep the chest out and the waist up in the crouching stance with the right leg horizontally straightened, the toes turned inward and the left leg bent to form a full squat. (Fig. 6-103)

图 6-103　仆步抢劈拳
Fig. 6-103 Swing and Chop Fist in a Crouching Stance

32. 提膝挑掌　　　　　　　　　　　　　　Uplift Palm with Knee Raised

要点： 立圆抢臂，提膝过腰，支撑稳定。（图6-104）

Key Points: Swing the arms in a vertical circle, raise the knee over the waist, and keep the support stable. (Fig. 6-104)

图 6-104　提膝挑掌
Fig. 6-104 Uplift Palm with Knee Raised

33. 提膝劈掌弓步冲拳

Uplift Knee with Palm Hacking and
Punch Fist in a Bow Stance

要点：下劈掌力达掌外沿；右弓步时右膝与脚面垂直，大腿呈水平位，左脚尖内扣，左膝蹬直；冲拳与弓步动作协调一致，力达拳面。（图6-105）

Key Points: The force of downward hacking reaches the outer edge of the palm; the right knee is perpendicular to the instep in right bow stance with the thigh at horizontal level; turn the left toes inward and straighten the left knee; keep the punching and bow stance coordinated, with the force reaching the face of fist. (Fig. 6-105)

图 6-105　提膝劈掌弓步冲拳
Fig. 6-105 Uplift Knee with Palm Hacking and Punch Fist in a Bow Stance

34. 收势 Closing Posture

（1）虚步亮掌

要点：右掌在头上方抖腕亮掌；左虚步时重心落于右腿，大腿呈水平位，左腿微屈，脚尖点地；虚步、亮掌、摆头动作协调一致。（图6-106）

(1) Show Palm in an Empty Stance

Key Points: Shake the wrist and show the palm above the head with the right palm; the center of gravity falls onto the right leg in a left empty stance with the thigh at horizontal level; slightly bend the left leg with the toes touching the ground; keep the empty stance, palm showing and head turning well coordinated. (Fig. 6-106)

图 6-106 虚步亮掌
Fig. 6-106 Show Palm in an Empty Stance

（2）并步对拳

要点：退步与前穿掌协调配合；并步、按拳与摆头同时完成，上下肢动作配合协调一致。（图6-107）

(2) Stand with Feet Together and Fist to Fist

Key Points: Keep the backward step and the forward Thrusting Palm coordinated, complete the folding stance (feet together), fist pressing and head turning at the same time, and keep the movements of upper and lower limbs coordinated. (Fig. 6-107)

图 6-107　并步对拳
Fig. 6-107 Stand with Feet Together and Fist to Fist

练习三段长拳结束后行抱拳礼。

At the end of your practice, perform the palm-fist salute.